How To Successfully Publish A Book On Amazon & Audible:

How To Build A Profitable Self-Publishing Business

Richard Abbott

Table of content

Introduction

I have been a self-publisher on amazon and audible for over a year now, and I have successfully made it a nice second income that I can rely on. In this book, I plan to show you how anybody can get started with self-publishing today and make it a side hustle. Self-publishing can also become a full-time occupation depending on how hard you work and how seriously you take this business.

This book will take you from A-Z in self-publishing. From finding the correct keywords all the way to getting your cover design made and book published on KDP.

Many people think that you need thousands of dollars to get started with self-publishing and that it is simply "too competitive" in 2022. This could not be further from the truth. Yes, while low content publishing is pretty competitive, there is still a great opportunity for high content publishing in the fiction and non-fiction space.

Every month I come across a dozen of untapped keywords that have low competition and high demand. I plan to show you how to find these keywords and write a great book that makes you passive income on amazon month after month.

Don't worry if you are not a writer! I will show you how to outsource your book to professional ghostwriters on Upwork for a fair price. You don't need thousands of dollars to get started. You can write a good quality book for a few hundred dollars.

Audiobooks are my favorite income stream as they are totally passive. Once you write a great book and have it ranking on audible, you can expect to get paid for months and years to come. Want to know the best part? There are no ads on audible, meaning that what we earn is pure profit!

I have tried a lot of online business models, and I can confidently say that this is by far the most beginner-friendly and rewarding business model today. Self-publishers earn 60-70% profit margins on paperbacks sold. This is something practically unheard of in e-commerce or even affiliate marketing. The best part about self-publishing is that there is no inventory, we utilize amazon's print-on-demand service, meaning that whenever we get an order, our books get printed and delivered by amazon, and we pocket the profits!

Essentially, you can decide to outsource nearly all the tasks in the self—publishing process, making this business model the true definition of passive income!

Chapter 1: Keyword Research

The most important part of self-publishing on amazon is keyword research. Without doing proper keyword research, you will end up making a few sales when you do release your book and get discouraged to continue publishing. Essentially, this is the make or break of your business and the foundation for your success to come.

I know what you might be thinking, "why can't I just write a book on a topic I am interested in" this is a good question and one that I had when I started as well. You see, the thing is, we chose keywords not based on what we think will sell well. We chose books based on the statistics and something that we call the best sellers rank (BSR).

Best Sellers Rank: #582,501 in Books (See Top 100 in Books)
#4,649 in Entrepreneurship (Books)

The best sellers rank (BSR) is on every Amazon product page when you scroll down towards the end of the page. Amazon uses this metric to differentiate between the best-selling products and the worst-selling products. The lower the BSR, the better for us because that means that the product is selling continuously.

When it comes to finding a good potential keyword for a book topic, we look for an average BSR of 150,000 and less. For e.g., if I were interested in the "affiliate marketing for beginners" keyword, this would need to have an average BSR rank of 150,000

Now that you understand the BSR function, it begs the question, how do you do keyword research?

The only tool that you need to do good keyword research is a tool called KDspy. It is a one-time tool that costs in the region of $60-70. This tool is an absolute must as it will save you a ton of time. I will show you how to use the tool in just a second.

Once you have purchased the KDspy tool, your next job is to find potential keywords to write books on.

Step 1 – The first step in this process is to go on the Amazon best sellers list for books. Make sure you are on the amazon.com marketplace and not any other!

This is what it should look like. As you can see on the side, ivt has all of the different categories. This is what we refer to in publishing as "niches." A niche is for, e.g., business & money, health fitness & dieting, or education & teaching. A keyword is a topic within one of those niches. I would recommend you to click on a niche that you are interested in. This is because if you are interested in a niche, you will be more motivated to produce the highest quality book. You will also have great insight into the topic and potentially have some physical experience that you can share with your readers.

Let's say, for example, I pick out business & money. That would be my overarching niche. A keyword within business & money could be, for example, accounting, affiliate marketing, entrepreneurship, etc. All of these keywords fall under the niche "money and finance."

Once you have clicked on the one you are interested in, it will show you the 100 best-selling books in that department. We want to skim through these book titles and find potential topics that we can write a book on ourselves. The reason why this strategy is so effective is that we are already at the best-selling books, so we don't have to worry about the demand for the books. The demand is there. Now it is our job to find the topic that suits us and one that we can potentially build a brand around.

Step 2 – Once you have come across a few book topics that you are interested in, you want to put them in an excel spreadsheet that looks something like this:

Niches & Keywords			Judging criteria		
Surface level niche	Sub level niche	Keyword	5-10 Similar results?	Avg BSR 150k or lower?	4000 results or less?
Business & money	Job hunting & careers	cracking the PM interview	Y	N	N
Business & money	Investing	A beginners guide to the stock market	Y	Y	Y

As you can see, there Is a section for the surface-level niche. In this example, it is business & money. The sub-level niche in this example is job hunting & careers. The keyword is cracking the pm interview, or how to successfully interview for a job.

Once we have a few of them down, we want to move on to the judging criteria. By following the above judging criteria, it will give you a good idea of whether or not this is a book worth perusing.

The first judging criteria is seeing whether there are 5-10 similar books with similar book titles on amazon.com (make sure you are on books). When I say similar, I mean that you can get a gist of what the book is about by reading the title of the book. If there are 5-10 similar books on interviewing, then it ticks the box for this criteria. The answer is yes.

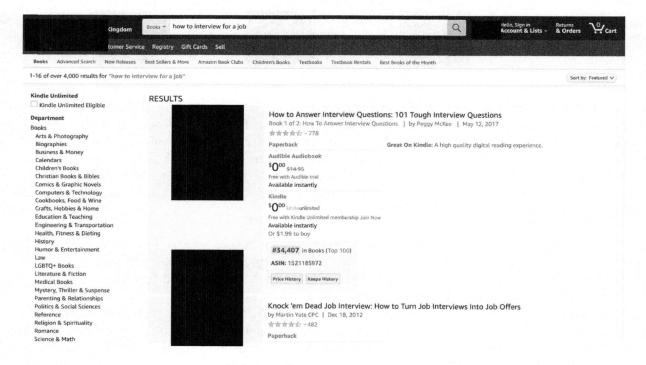

The next step in the criteria is seeing whether or not the keyword has an average best sellers rank on amazon.com of at least 150,000. It would be ideal if it were lower than that. However, the average BSR rank is 150,000.

How we would do this is to go to our google extensions and click on the KDspy extension, it will automatically generate the statistics you can see below.

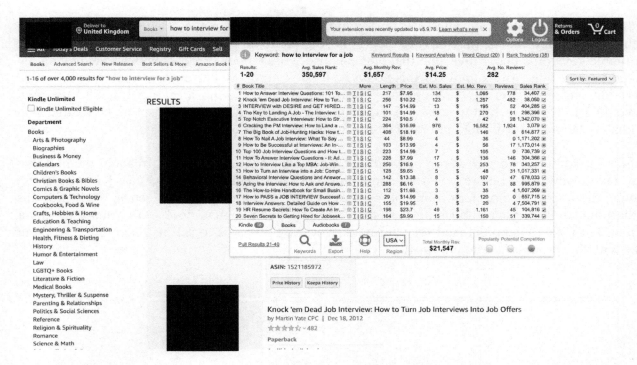

As you can see, the average BSR for this keyword is 350,000, this is a bit high, and therefore we would go back to our criteria and make sure to write "no" for this criteria. How the average BSR is calculated is by adding up all of the best seller ranks on the first page and then dividing it by the number of books on the first page. As you can imagine, this can be a tedious job if you are going through a potential hundred keywords. Therefore, it is very important that you buy this one-time tool, as it will save you a lot of money!

The last criteria that we look at are seeing whether there are 4000 results or less on the amazon.com marketplace for this keyword. The answer to the one I used for an example was yes, so you would go back to your spreadsheet and write "yes." The reason why we try to stick to 4000 and less is that anything more than that will be hard to compete with and hard to rank on the first page. The goal is to eventually rank our books on the first page of amazon as it means that we will later down the line not have to rely on amazon ads to generate sales. If a keyword has more than 4000 results, there will likely be too much competition, and this will therefore be very difficult.

Those are the main steps I take in finding profitable keywords. We want to try and build a authority and a brand, so go with a niche that you are passionate about and that you have some sort of background in (as long as it passes the above criteria, of course).

One thing to also note is that we will try to create multiple books in our surface-level niche, as this will help with brand building instead of publishing one book in one niche and then moving on to the other. Doing that will not help you to really build an audience and an email list that will eventually become loyal customers.

Let's say, for example, I am interested in the money and finance niche. That is the surface-level niche. The sub-level niche may be investing. It is your job to now make sure that there are multiple profitable keywords under investing that you can also write a book on. This is because they are all linked to investing. An example of this could be a book on cryptocurrency, a book on real estate investing, and a book on NFTs. All of the keywords fall under the sub-level niche that is investing. It would be helpful to find at least 3-5 profitable keywords under a sub-level niche as that will ultimately help us in building our brand with a few books under our author page.

This is the only keyword research method that I personally use. Yes, it is a manual method that may take a few days before you find something that you really like. However, I cannot stress enough the importance of performing proper keyword research with due diligence. As I said, this is the foundation of your publishing business. You can create a great book with a fantastic cover design, but if there is no demand for your book, you won't be able to sell it. Therefore, take your time with this process and do not rush!

Special Bonus

Want this bonus book for FREE?

Get FREE access to it and all of my new books by joining the fan base

Scan W/ Your Camera To Join!

Chapter 2: Book Outline

After you have successfully chosen a niche and your first keyword, it is now time to write a book outline. A book outline is very important because, without one, we would be letting our ghostwriters write freely and without any strict guidelines and instructions to follow. Based on my personal experience, this is not something that you want to do because they will end up not taking your project very seriously.

I like to be very specific with my book outlines. They sometimes exceed 4,000 words! Now you don't have to make them that long, that is just a personal preference, but you could do it if you wanted!

In this chapter, I won't show you the exact book outline that I use. However, I will tell you everything that needs to be included in a book outline.

I start my book outlines by making it very clear to the writers that I take the quality of my books seriously and that I will not move on until I am satisfied with them. I then tell them that this was a team effort and that if there was anything that they did not understand in the outline, for them to get in touch with me.

Here I am just setting the expectations high, so my writers know that slacking on my projects will not be tolerated. I would definitely recommend that you start your book outlines with something similar to this.

After that, I let the writer know that the book outline will be centered around five main points, they are:

- **Information** – I stress to the writers the importance of using reliable and correct information.

- **The focus** – I stress to the writer the importance of not including any fluff in my book to merely make up the word count.

- **Organization** – I stress to my writer the importance of following the chapter outlines and making sure everything is in a logical and organized manner.

- **The flow** – I stress to the writer the importance of making sure that each chapter flows nicely into the next one and that they should be linked.

- **Language** – I stress the importance of using language that reflects the target age of the book.

After I have made that clear to the writer, I then have a filled-out section. You will need to include the following information to your writer:

- Book title –

- Book subtitle –

- Author –

- Word count –

- Target Audience –

- Gender –

- Age –

- The main problems the readers are currently facing –

- The solution to their problems -

It is important that you provide this information to the writer BEFORE they start working on your book. The reason for this is because by them having a good idea of your target audience's demographics, they will have a good idea of the writing style and flow of the book. It is also important that you make it clear to the writer the type of writing style you are going with. Is it a juvenile writing style, or more for adults? All of this information must be made very clear to the ghostwriter.

The reason why we make a list of the readers' main problems and solutions for them is so that the writer writes in a way where they can tackle those main points. If you hire a writer who actually has physical experience in your keyword (which I highly recommend), they will likely already know the readers' main problems; however, it is always good to remind the writer of them, so they keep them in mind when writing the bodying chapters of your book.

The next stage in the book outline is the Introduction. I make it very clear to the writer that the Introduction is the most important section of the book because if a potential reader reads the Introduction and is not moved by it, they will likely not go any further with reading your book. However, if they like your Introduction, the majority of times, you will find that they will purchase your book and want to read more.

Before I give them any information in regards to what to write for the Introduction, I list the top 5 best-selling books in that particular keyword. I do this as it will help the writer to curate a great book introduction. I make it very clear to the writer that they are not to copy any work but simply take ideas and inspiration from the best-selling books that are already selling well.

I then proceed to mention to the writer that the Introduction should be in this particular order:

1. The writer should start by identifying and stating the problem. The reason why the customer picked up this book is that they want to know how the book will solve their problems.

2. The writer should then present the solution to the reader. The writer should explain why this book is the solution to their problem.

3. I then ask the writer to assert some credibility and why they are qualified to help them solve their problems. This is one of the main reasons why I work with writers that do not solely have research experience but also physical experience in the field. This will help to assert credibility and build trust with the reader that you are the perfect person to help them with their worries and concerns. I often ask writers to briefly include their qualifications and experience in this section of the Introduction.

4. I then ask the writer to write up the benefits of our book and how reading our book will change the reader's situation for the better.

5. I then ask the writer to present proof of their credibility in the form of case studies. A good example of this would be if you were writing a workout book, you could include case studies of the results of your previous clients. Readers like this would be a lot more likely to purchase your book if you included credible case studies.

6. The writer should then make a promise to the reader that at the end of reading the book, they will be confident in tackling their main issues. Making a promise is great but don't overpromise and underdeliver.

7. Towards the end of the Introduction, I ask the writer to create a sense of urgency. This should be written in a way where the readers would feel guilty if they did not pick up your book now.

8. Lastly, I tell my writer to end the Introduction with a call to action. I ask the writer to hint at some juicy secrets that our book will reveal should they purchase it. Maybe write an interesting fact or statistic surrounding your topic, something that will grab their attention. It is important that we do not sell our whole book through the Introduction. Rather, the reader should want to read more after reading the intro. They should not feel like they already know what your book will contain inside.

That is the end of the Introduction of the book. The Introduction will usually range from 1000-2000 words. Anything more than that is too long. Slightly shorter than 1000 is fine.

We then get to the main bodying chapters of the book. I like to stick to 7-9 chapters, excluding the conclusion. This is for an average 30,000-word book. If you plan to write a longer book, this would, of course, increase.

How do I come up with the bodying chapters?

This is a very good question, and this stage of my book outline usually takes me the most amount of time.

This is also another reason why I highly recommend you to choose a niche and keyword that you are interested in, provided that it is, of course, profitable and has demand. This is because if you don't, you will skim over this part of the outline as you will not be motivated to do the research. Yes, this part will require a lot of research!

The first way in which we will get ideas of the main bodying chapters is by simply reading the table of contents for the best sellers on the first page for your keyword. The purpose of this is not to copy, but again, it's to take inspiration and see what sort of topics should be covered in the main bodying chapters.

One of the main ways I come up with topics for the main bodying chapters is through reading three-star reviews for books on the first page. The reason why I say three stars and not four or five is because customers who leave three-star reviews usually leave a detailed review that has elements of both praise and areas for improvement. Also, these reviews usually highlight the main pain points of the customers, so if you do not happen to know them already, you can find them here.

I will read ALL of the three-star reviews for my competitors' books, yes, this may be a slightly tedious task, but it will surely be worth it. Make a list of the main important points that you took from each review and jot down ideas for chapter outlines based on where the other author missed out on.

This is also a great incentive for those readers to purchase your book over your competition. Not only will your book be more up to date but in terms of information and statistics, but it will also answer and fill the void of other factors that your competitors could not do. When your readers see your table of contents, they will be more likely to pick out your book.

Once you have a good idea of what the bodying chapters will be, it is a good practice to double-check that each chapter is flowing nicely from one chapter to the other. They should be relevant and possibly be linked to each other if possible.

I try to stick to four to five main points that need to be addressed within each chapter. Again, make sure you put them in an appropriate order and make sure that each point is relevant to the chapter.

References are very important to me, and you should also take them very seriously. I make a list of references that I want the writer to use for each point within the chapter. I do this to prevent the writer from using unreliable resources in the book. It is important that you first find good resources that are credible and that you pass them over to your writer. I try to stick to academic resources and other books and newspaper articles for my main references.

With that being said, I do make it clear to the writer that I am not totally against them using their own resources, but they would have to verify the source with me first before using it for the book.

All of the above and everything I have said until this point is targeted for non-fiction books, but this can also be applicable to fiction books. I personally don't have any experience in this field. However, if you do, you can follow the same steps to come up with the book outline.

Chapter 3: To Write Yourself Or Outsource? Upwork Or A Ghostwriting Company?

At this stage, you should have now finished the outline for your book. It's now time to decide whether you outsource your book or write it yourself. If you chose a niche that you are really passionate about and that is profitable, I would highly recommend you to write your first book yourself. Don't worry too much about grammar and punctuation, as we will use a tool that I will discuss in the next chapter to help you with that.

Another good reason why it would make sense to write your first book yourself is so that you can get an idea of how ghostwriting is so that you go into your first ghostwritten book with a ghostwriter with the right expectations.

With that said, if you chose a niche that you are not the most passionate about and you consider yourself to be a rookie writer, it would make sense to outsource your first book to a ghostwriter or a ghostwriting company.

If you just want to get your fingers wet with this new business model and you are not sure if it will work out for you, it would make sense to write the book yourself. However, bear in mind that your major expense will be your time, so if you are happy to risk your time, and you would rather do that than spend a few hundred bucks, go ahead and write your book.

Before we go into Upwork and ghostwriting companies, it is important to realize that if you outsource your book or if you write it yourself, it will still roughly take the same amount of time to complete; therefore, don't feel the need to rush your book, you would much rather spend a little longer but have a really high-quality book that sells well on Amazon for years, rather than a rushed book with a lot of mistakes and poor-quality writing. Based on my experience of over a dozen books, a 30,000-word book takes around 3-4 weeks for most ghostwriters to finish. If you are writing a book for the first time, four weeks is a reasonable deadline to set for yourself. When we break this down, it is about 2000 words that you would have to type up every day. If you have attended university, college, or any educational institute and you are used to using Microsoft word, we can all agree that this is totally doable. Even if you are currently working full time, this is achievable. Simply set out an hour to ninety minutes every day where you are focused on your laptop. Within a month, you will hopefully see the fruits of your labor.

Ghostwriting companies

Ok, if you have now decided that you simply don't have the capacity to write your own book and that you will outsource it, using a ghostwriting company is a viable option that you can explore.

There are many ghostwriting companies, and prices will vary greatly. The ghostwriting companies that I can hand on heart recommend are:

- The Hot Ghostwriter

- The Urban Writers
- The Writing Summit

The Hot Ghostwriters

The hot ghostwriter is the most expensive out of the three listed above, although it also does have the reputation and reviews on Trustpilot.

With the hot ghostwriters, you can expect to pay around $1500 for a 30,000-word book, they are by no means cheap, so if you are on a limited budget, I would advise looking elsewhere.

If you do have the money, though, you can have a piece of mind that they will produce the best possible work you. The hot ghostwriters have a wide range of writers that specialize in various niches and keywords. Once they receive your submission requirements, they will assign your task to the writer they deem to be fittest for the work. I am also aware that they have recently updated how writers and clients keep in contact during the production of the book. Before, it was not ideal in the sense that you would place an order and not hear back until it was time to deliver your work. Now, however, they have a system where you can constantly keep in touch with your writer and check in with them to see how the work is progressing. This is great!

As for the urban writers, if you go for their most expensive package, that is the "premium package," you could expect to pay around $1100 for a 30,000-word book. This one is $400 cheaper than the hot ghostwriters. I can't tell you which ghostwriting company is the best because each project is different and has different requirements. It's a matter of testing and seeing which one you prefer and is most suited to your requirements.

As for the writing summit, their best package, which is the "top writer" package, costs $3 per 100 words so a 30,000-word book would set you back $900. They are the cheapest out of the three, but they are also one of the newer companies as well, which is something to take into consideration.

Overall, it's a matter of weighing up your options and making a decision. Make sure you also ask each company to give you a sample of work that is preferably similar to the type of book you want to be written. This will give you a better idea of whether they would be suitable for you or not.

Advantages of ghostwriting companies

- Peace of mind that you will get back a high-quality book

- You will save a lot of time as you won't need to vet out candidates yourself

Disadvantages of ghostwriting companies

- They cost significantly more than hiring a freelancer.

- You lack that 1-to-1 communication with the writer with most ghostwriting companies.

- Some ghostwriting companies can ghost you and not respond for a few days/weeks, depending on how busy they are with existing projects.

- You don't really know how many other projects your projected writer is juggling alongside your book. This is bad because they could be overwhelmed with a lot of work, causing the quality of your final submission to suffer as they have to juggle a lot of projects.

As you can tell, the disadvantages outweigh the advantages. I personally would not recommend you to go through a ghostwriting company for the above reasons.

I will now compare this to the freelancing platform Upwork

Upwork

Upwork is a freelancing platform that has millions of freelancers who freelance for clients. With Upwork, you have a lot more flexibility in terms of the prices you wish to pay.

How it works is that you post a job, and then writers will apply with interest. In my opinion, this is by far the best freelancing platform as they have the highest quality freelancers. Fiverr is fine for cover design and other tasks, but from my experience, they have low-quality writers.

Another reason why I believe Upwork is a lot better than Fiverr is that, on Upwork, you post the job, and freelancers apply, meaning that people are genuinely interested in working with you. Whereas on Fiverr, you do not have this privilege, on Fiverr, you have to personally reach out to freelancers and writers to enquire about your project. In this scenario, you lose a lot of leverage because a lot of the time, you will find that writers on Fiverr already have their prices and their strict requirements on their profile, leaving you with little to bargain over.

On the other hand, Upwork is very open in the sense that you can negotiate with writers a lot more.

On Upwork, I never really pay more than $400 for a high-quality 30,000-word book. This is a writer who has not only research experience on the topic but also practical experience.

As you can see, you will save a lot more money compared to going with a ghostwriting company. With that being said, because you are personally hiring your writer, you will need to vet all the individuals who apply to your job posting.

Whenever I usually post a job advert for a ghostwriter on Upwork, I usually get at least 30/40 writers who show interest. Going through all of these applicants alone can take many hours as you have to go through samples of each applicant and speak to them a bit further.

Below is the job posting that I use every time. Feel free to take it and use it for yourself:

'Hi, there!

My name is …

We run a book publishing company on amazon. We publish 2 To 3 high-quality non-fiction books on a monthly basis. We are currently searching for a highly talented, meticulous, and detail-orientated writer to join our team on a long-term basis.

We are looking for a Ghostwriter to join our team to help us dominate the… (INSERT YOUR NICHE HERE) niche. Below are the responsibilities for this role. Please be sure to apply with your recent work and preferably work of a similar nature topic/niche.

- Extensive experience in the … (insert niche) niche. Both research-based and personal experience.
- Create original (copyright-free) and engaging content of 30k words (or however much you want to write)
- Conversationally fluent in the English language.
- Have great attention to detail for quality work.
- A person who meets deadlines (very important)
- A person who is easily reachable and highly responsive via the Upwork messenger platform.
- Books need to be proofread before final submission.
- You have to be open and willing to take criticism.

The specific topic that we are looking to have this book written on is (ENTER YOUR KEYWORD HERE)

Please apply with your previous work, as well as a few sentences explaining why you think you are suitable for this role.

QUESTIONS TO ADD IN (UPWORK)

- What is your experience with the (enter your niche) niche?
- What is your experience writing informative content on this topic of 30k words and upwards?
- How long would it take you to complete this type of project?

We look forward to hearing from you again.'

With a detailed job posting like this, you will no doubt find high-quality ghostwriters who will be happy to work with you.

If you are unaware of how to post a job on Upwork, follow the steps below. If you do not have an account on Upwork, make sure you sign up first, but make sure you sign up as a client, not a freelancer. This is important!

Step 1 – Click on where it says post a job.

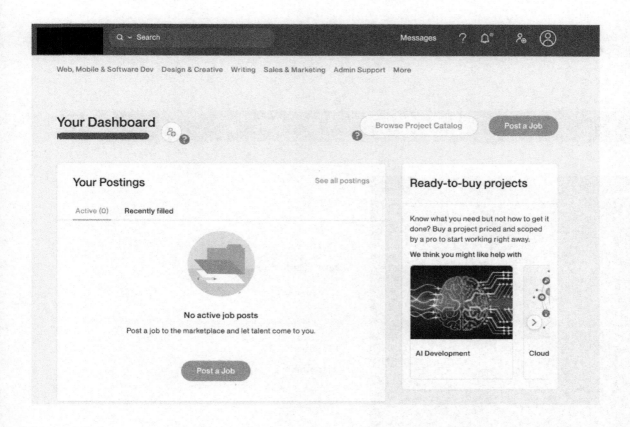

Step 2 – you will then be taken to a page that looks like this. Click on short-term or part-time work, then select continue.

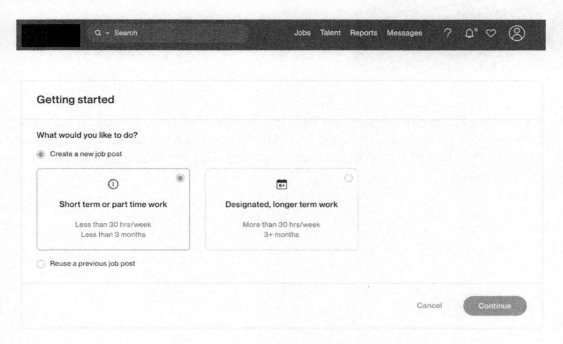

Step 3 – you will then be taken to a page like this, you can write something like "Ghostwriting for kindle book" as the job title, make sure you select the category as ghostwriting, then select "next: skills"

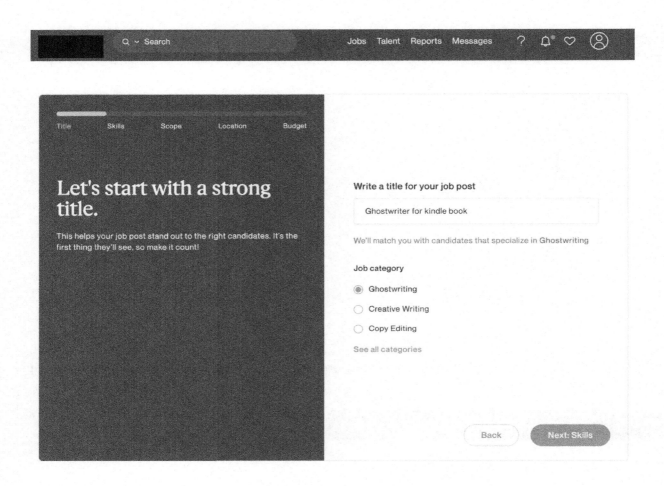

Step 4 – Now it's time to add ten skills. This will help freelancers find your posting as the skills will show to freelancers who possess the qualities you select here. I usually go with the popular skills, and that usually works fine for me. You can also pick out skills from the categories below as well, but they cannot surpass ten.

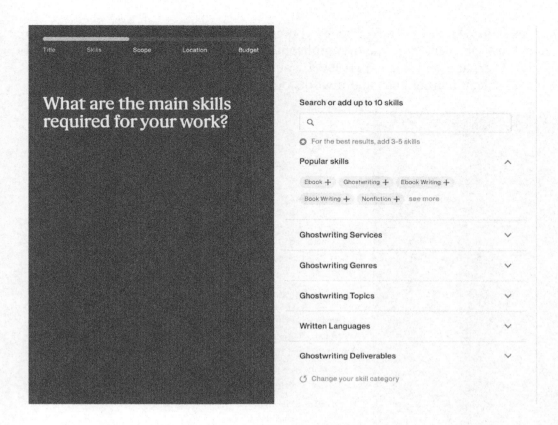

Step 5 – this page should appear next. It will ask us about the scope of the work. Make sure you select medium. For the question where it says, "how long will it take" you can select 1 to 3 months.

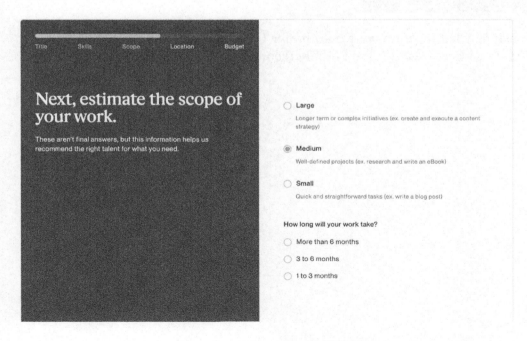

Step 6 – It will now ask you what level of experience you need the freelancer to have. I usually go for intermediate, and I still get very high-quality applicants. I don't go for entry as I have found that the applicants are fewer, and with the expert level, you would have to spend a lot higher than $400; therefore, I like to select intermediate, and it works out very well for me.

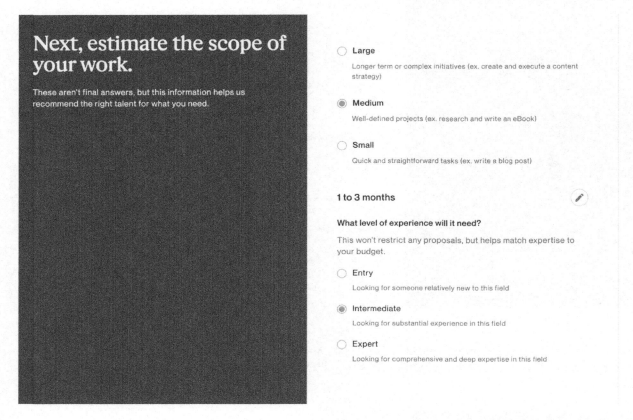

Step 7 – It will then ask us what location we would prefer Ghostwriters to be from. I like to keep my options broad, so I go with worldwide, and I highly recommend that you do the same.

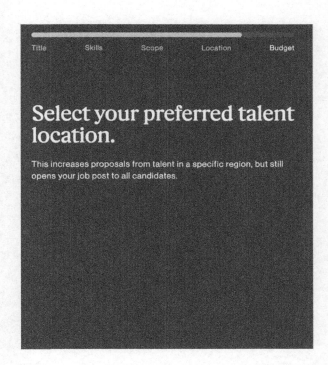

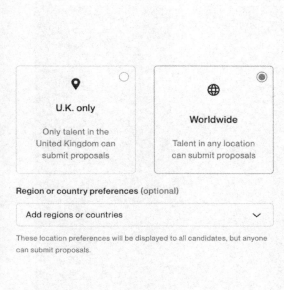

Step 8 – we are now at one of the last stages. Here is where you will set your budget for your role. Do not make the mistake and select an hourly rate. This is because you never really know how many hours the freelancer might take to finish writing your book, so you could be paying well over $400 for the book. Because of this reason, I like to stick to a project budget of $400. This gives me peace of mind to know that the price of the project will not increase regardless of how long it takes. Then click on the review job post.

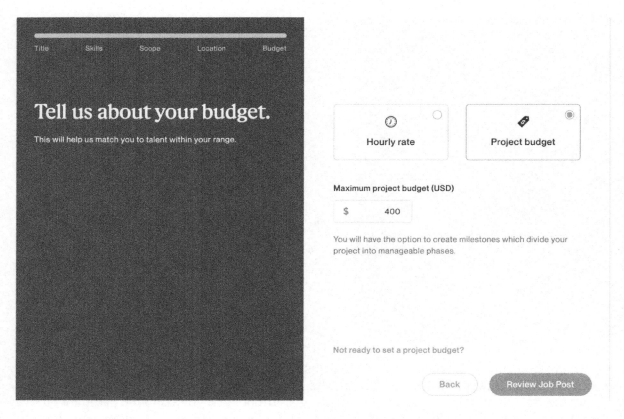

Tell us about your budget.

This will help us match you to talent within your range.

Hourly rate

Project budget

Maximum project budget (USD)

$ 400

You will have the option to create milestones which divide your project into manageable phases.

Not ready to set a project budget?

Back   Review Job Post

Step 9 – this is now the last stage before you post your job. Take the job description template above and paste it here. When you scroll down on this last page, you will also have the option to add the screening questions.

Now just finish and review your job post.

[Post Your Job Now]

Title

Ghostwriter for kindle book

Describe your job

This is how talent figures out what you need and why you're great to work with!

Include your expectations about the task or deliverable, what you're looking for in a work relationship, and anything unique about your project, team, or company. Here are several examples that illustrate best practices for effective job posts.

> • A person who is easily reachable and highly responsive via the Upwork messenger platform.
> • Books need to be proofread before final submission.
> • You have to be open and willing to take criticism
>
> The specific topic that we are looking to have this book written on is (ENTER YOUR KEYWORD HERE)
>
> Please apply with your previous work as well as a few sentences explaining why you think you are suitable for this role.
>
> QUESTIONS TO ADD IN (UPWORK)
>
> • What is your experience with the (enter your niche) niche?
> • What is your experience writing informative content on this topic of 30k words and upwards?
> • How long would it take you to complete this type of project?
>
> We look forward to hearing from you again.'

3409 characters left

You are now done. Your job post is now live and ready for people to apply.

Congratulations! Your job post is now live.

Upwork tips and tricks

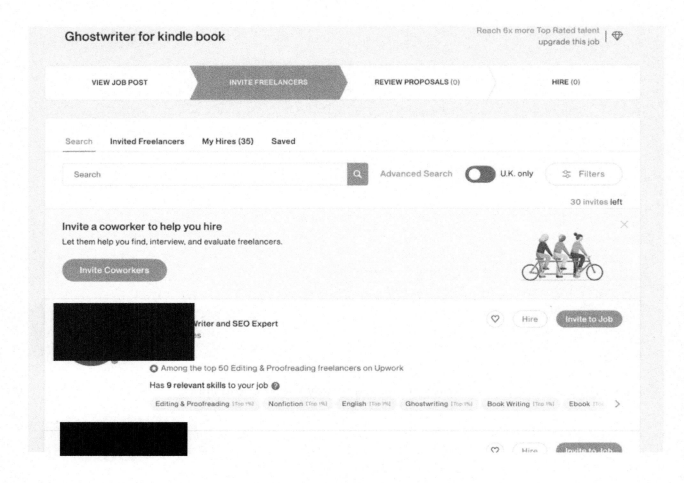

Once you have posted your job on Upwork, the screen will look something like this. When you sign up for a free client account on Upwork, you have the ability to invite 30 candidates for free. This is very helpful because even though you will get plenty of applicants organically, inviting another 30 will surely give you more options. There are also filters. I recommend that you filter it out where it only shows you writers that have earned over $10k on Upwork. This shows us that they have done quite a few ghostwriting projects already and that they are experienced. I also recommend that you filter it out so that it shows candidates with at least 95% job success. This shows that the freelancer has received great feedback from previous clients and gives us peace of mind that they are punctual and will complete the project.

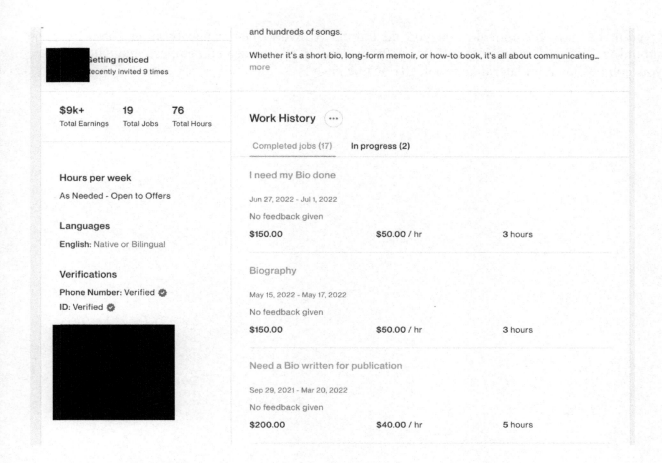

and hundreds of songs.

Whether it's a short bio, long-form memoir, or how-to book, it's all about communicating...
more

$9k+   **19**   **76**
Total Earnings   Total Jobs   Total Hours

Hours per week

As Needed - Open to Offers

Languages

English: Native or Bilingual

Verifications

Phone Number: Verified
ID: Verified

Work History ...

Completed jobs (17)   **In progress (2)**

I need my Bio done

Jun 27, 2022 - Jul 1, 2022

No feedback given

$150.00 $50.00 / hr   3 hours

Biography

May 15, 2022 - May 17, 2022

No feedback given

$150.00 $50.00 / hr   3 hours

Need a Bio written for publication

Sep 29, 2021 - Mar 20, 2022

No feedback given

$200.00 $40.00 / hr   5 hours

Another thing that I really like about Upwork is that when you click on your applicants' profiles, you can see their complete jobs and how many jobs they have currently in progress. This is very important because we don't want to work with a writer that already has a lot on their plate. I recommend that you don't work with a freelancer that has more than three current projects in progress. Anything more than three will likely mean that the quality of your work will decrease.

Upwork advantages

- Significantly cheaper than going through a ghostwriting company
- You can find higher quality writers than on ghostwriting companies
- You can schedule zoom meetings and 1 to 1's with the writer and properly vet them yourself

Upwork disadvantages

- It can be very time-consuming to vet the correct candidate. It can sometimes take days on end.
- No guarantee that you will receive satisfying work like with ghostwriting companies. It can be hit or miss if you don't vet candidates properly.

Overall, I highly recommend that you go through Upwork over a ghostwriting company. You should wait at least a few days to start vetting candidates because sometimes candidates can see your job posting a bit later than usual, so don't be hasty!

Chapter 4: Cover Design, Book Title, And Book Description

Cover design is up there among the most important steps in the publishing process.

Essentially, the first thing that your potential customer will see on amazon and audible is your title and cover design. The attention span of customers is very short, so if you fail to grab their attention with your cover design, they will likely continue scrolling and look at other books.

I highly recommend that you spend at least $50 on a quality graphic designer. Please avoid $5 gigs on Fiverr, as these covers are very low quality that will not sell very well.

There are some great gigs on Fiverr from $50 upwards for cover designers; however, I like to also go through Upwork for my cover design as I have full control over the price I set, my requirements, and deadlines.

What I like to do with my cover design is to put together a word document with the ideas that I want my designer to put into fruition. Make sure you have the book title, subtitle, and author name on your requirements very clearly. I also like to have at least five examples of cover designs and fonts that I like in the same niche and at least five that I do not like. By doing this, I am making it very clear to the graphic designer the theme that I like, so they can follow something different. I always try to put my own spin on my cover designs so that they stand out from my competition.

If you want to go through Upwork for your cover designer, simply post a similar job listing to the job description for the Ghostwriter. Make sure you ask for enough sample cover designs, so you can see if the cover designer is suitable for you or not.

Let us go over what makes a good cover design in comparison to a poor one that will not generate a consistent stream of income.

Let's have a look at two covers in the same niche, just to make things fair.

Cover 1 - "Developing Emotional Intelligence: 30 Ways For Older Teens And Young Adults to Develop Their Caring Capabilities Volume 5 By Israelin Shockness"

This is the first cover in the emotional intelligence keyword. In my opinion, this cover looks very dull and boring. It looks similar to all the other covers on emotional intelligence in the kindle store. It does not have that wow factor or an element that would make me pick this book up over others. I don't like the background image, and while it mixes nicely with the white text and font, I don't see how it is relevant to the topic of emotional intelligence.

Cover 2 – "EQ Applied: The Real-World Guide To Emotional Intelligence. How To Make Emotions Work For You, Instead Of Against You"

This is the 2nd cover in the same keyword. In my opinion, this cover looks a lot more appealing. It looks different from other covers in the same keyword. I like how the designer has incorporated the sculpture within the letter "Q" and also the colors and bubbles around it. The background is also appealing as it really brings the cover out to the viewer.

You do not need to re-invent the wheel to create an appealing cover, nor do you need to pay over $50, in my opinion. It is all about having a certain element of your cover that sticks out and separates you from your competitors, whether that is the background, an illustration that is only on your cover, or something else. Customers are a lot more likely to remember this cover than the first one.

Let's have a look at another example in a different keyword.

Cover 1: "Overthinking" – Daniel Michael

This cover is in the overthinking keyword. I don't think this cover is as bad as the first one; however, when you see the competitors, it is really no competition.

Cover 2 – "Stop Overthinking: 23 Techniques To Relieve Stress, Stop Negative Spirals, Declutter Your Mind, And Focus On The Present By Nick Trenton"

As you can see, this cover stands out a lot more and is a lot more unique. The orange background really grabs your attention. The main element in this cover is the outline of the head, the cover designer used words and sentences to make this up, and it looks very unique and eye-catching. It will be very hard to come across a cover similar to this on amazon, and therefore this cover is more attractive to the customer.

So just to round up what I have already mentioned, the following is what you need to consider to have an attractive book cover:

• Have a good idea of a design concept/s that you would like – Send your freelancer everything you can to make their life easier. For e.g., other covers you like, fonts you like, colors you like and dislike, etc.

• Consider how your book cover would look on a bookshelf. Would you buy it if you came across it?

• Make sure that you have a unique idea that stands out from competitors.

• Make sure that your idea is easy on the eyes. It should not have too many elements, fancy fonts, colors, etc.

• Don't give away your book with your cover. Leave some thoughts to be thought about.

Things to take into consideration when ordering your cover for the first time

I always only order the eBook cover design only from the graphic designer. There are a few reasons for this:

1. You don't know if you will like the graphic designer's final cover or not. Therefore, you would be wasting money if you ordered the eBook, paperback, and audiobook cover.

2. It's a lot cheaper just to order the eBook cover and then get it transformed into paperback and audiobook in a separate gig. These gigs are very cheap on Fiverr, in the range of $5-$10. However, if you order all three from your cover designer, you will pay at least another $30-40.

3. The ideal dimensions for your e-book cover will be 2560 pixels x 1600 pixels. Make sure you mention this to the graphic designer.

Once you have your e-book cover back and you are happy with it, It is now time to get the paperback version designed. You will need to give the following specifications to another designer:

• The page count of your book – Take the page count from the PDF of your book

• The ink and paper type – best to go for a black and white interior unless you have a book with many illustrations or a book with loads of images and charts.

• Trim size – will mostly be 6 x 9 or 5 x 8

• Paperback cover finish – will it be matte or glossy?

• The blurb description – I usually take this from the book description; however, you can come up with something new if you would like to.

• Is there something specific that you want to be written on the spine?

Book title/subtitle

A title is one of the most important stages in the publishing process.

• Avoid a first draft book title and aim for a second draft book title.

• A bad book title can negatively affect your sales and make your book unattractive to your audience – make sure your title stands out from the crowd.

• DO NOT keyword stuff your title (first draft book title) as your potential audience will not like it, and it will come across as spammy.

That then begs the question, what is a first draft book title?

For Example: "Emotional Intelligence For Leadership: Improve Your Skills To Succeed In Business, Manage People, and Become A Great Leader – Boost Your EQ And Improve Social Skills, Self-Awareness, Charisma By Dr. Louise Lily Wain"

This is an example of a first draft book title.

• The title is very basic.

• A lot of keyword stuffing is going on here.

• Subtitle is too long.

• Title is not flowy, literally something you would search up on the search engines.

• Comes off as spammy in the eyes of the customer. They will likely move on to the next book.

• Uncomfortable to say out loud.

• Too vague, does not spark any interest or controversy.

• Lack of originality. The title does not stick out from the competitors.

Now that you know what a first book title is and to avoid it. Let's now look at a second draft book title:

For example: Emotional Intelligence For The Modern Leader: A Guide To Cultivating Effective Leadership And Organizations By Christopher D. Connors"

• The title is a lot more creative.

• The title sounds & flows better.

• Still targeting emotional intelligence for leadership, but this one does not stuff in as many keywords as possible.

• Less spammy.

• Peaks more interest.

• More appealing.

• Sticks out from the crowd.

Make sure the following is present when choosing your book title:

• Title is informative yet straight to the point and hooks the buyer – NO keyword stuffing.

• The title should not be embarrassing or have any offensive remarks in it.

• The title should have some form of controversy – It should make the potential buyer want to pick it up and read more. Don't play it safe like with the first draft cover example.

• The title should be flowy and also brandable.

• Keep the title within five words if possible – this is because the cover will look better aesthetically as there will be more space on the cover.

• The title MUST include your keyword in there one way or the other. It's your job to include it in a creative way.

• The subtitle can be a bit longer but not too long. The subtitle serves to articulate what you could not do with your main keyword in the title.

For example: "Why Does He Do That? Inside The Minds Of Angry And Controlling Men By Lundy Bancroft"

This is a great example of my last point on the subtitle.

• Has a bit of controversy – but not too controversial to the point where you would be embarrassed to discuss it in public with friends and family.

• The title vaguely states the purpose of the book – again, it sparks interest.

The subtitle:

• Confirms the main keyword of this title and what the book is about.

• Is not too long, yet it perfectly sums up the topic of the book.

• Is visually appealing.

Pen name/ author name

Your pen/ author's name is the author of your book. I never use my own name for my author's name because of the following reasons:

- I am in a few niches, so I like to keep one pen name to one niche. Think about it, is it realistic for someone to specialize in multiple niches?

- It's easier to build a brand around a fictional name based on my experience.

I use Reedy's pen name generator tool, but you can come up with one yourself.

Book description

The book description is also very important. The book description alongside your cover and title will have a big impact on the sales projection of your book.

Make sure the following are present when writing your book description.

• The first line or so should spark interest. I usually start it off with a rhetorical question.

• Make sure the book description focuses on the customer's pain points/ where they currently are in life and why your book is the answer to their problems.

• Make it clear that your book will answer their main problems.

• Briefly state your authority and experience with the topic.

• Keep the book description between 200-300 words.

• Keep it concise and short.

• Consider including some interesting facts, perhaps a bold claim or a story that will spike the potential reader's interest and make them want to read more.

• Your book description should be an ad for your book, NOT a summary. It's a sales pitch for your book.

Grammarly

If you are writing your book yourself or getting it outsourced, you will still have to read over it again and proofread it. This can be a tedious task that can sometimes take days, depending on how much time you spend on it.

This is why I use a tool called Grammarly. With Grammarly, you want to make sure you go for the business plan. The reason for this is because you will get the plagiarism checker within this plan, this is also very important as you need to run a plagiarism check before you publish any book, so you can be on the safe side that your book is 100% copyright free.

You will copy your book manuscript inside Grammarly. Grammarly then has three main sections that will allow you to improve your work. They are:

- Correctness – This is the section where you will probably spend the most time. Here it will highlight the grammar and punctuation errors in your manuscript, and you can very quickly update and correct them.

- Clarity – this section will help to make your writing easier to understand. Grammarly may suggest updates to your sentence structures etc.

- Engagement – this section will help to make your writing more interesting and effective.

- Delivery – this section helps you to make the right impression on your reader.

Overall, for about $12 a month, this tool is definitely worth it and will save you a lot of time and stress!

Chapter 5: Freebie funnel

A freebie funnel is something that looks like this:

SPECIAL BONUS!

Want this bonus book for **FREE?**

Get **FREE,** unlimited access to it and all of my new
books by joining the Fan Base!

Click here to join!

This is something you would most likely include at the beginning of your book or somewhere around the first chapter. Why is this effective?

You see, with Amazon, when a customer purchases our books, we get the sale. However, we never really know who the buyers are. With this funnel, we get the customer's email address in return for a free book. We usually offer a free book that is relevant to the main keyword of the book. For example, if the main book is on making money online, then this freebie offer book on the topic of side hustles is perfect as it links well with the topic.

When somebody knows and clicks on "click here to join," they will get taken to a landing page that looks like this.

Get Your Free... Book By Entering Your Email!

On top of that, plenty of others are already enjoying insider access to all of my current and future-length books, 100% free!

Join below today!

Email Address

First Name

Subscribe

All of this is free to create, and I will show you how to do this all now. However, before I do so, let's discuss some more benefits of having a freebie funnel like this inside your books:

• Get customers' emails – This is helpful because we can ask customers to leave us reviews on our books via email and sell them other products, i.e., affiliate marketing.

• Build a better connection with your customers over email.

• Build an ARC team in the future to help you generate reviews for your upcoming book. This is probably the biggest advantage of this freebie funnel.

An ARC team is a group of passionate fans of your author's name and books. They are a group of people (usually around 20) who will agree to read your book before it gets released to the public in exchange for a review when the book launches on Amazon.

This is very helpful as you will be off to a fantastic start when your book launches. This will also save you a lot of time for future book launches because, as you will come to see, getting reviews for your books can be a manual process that can be time-consuming, so once you have built up a decent email list, you can set up your own arc team, and they will help you with reviewing your book.

Just to clarify, we will generate two different freebie funnels for our book. The one you see above is for the eBook. Once they click on that link, they will be taken to the landing page.

The 2nd version will look something like this:

SPECIAL BONUS!

Want this book for FREE?

Get FREE, unlimited access to it and all of my new books by joining the Fan Base!

SCAN W/ YOUR CAMERA TO JOIN!

This is the paperback version, this version of the funnel will have a QR code instead of a link because this will be a printable book, so customers will not be able to click on it; instead, they will scan it with their smartphone camera, once they do, they will be taken to the same landing page on their phone.

Now that we have that out the way let me explain how we can create a funnel like this from scratch.

Step 1 – Create a free Gmail account for your author's name.

Let's say, for e.g., Your author's name is David Richard,
I would recommend you create a Gmail account with your author name + books @gmail.com

So, it would be Davidrichardbooks@gmail.com.

Of course, you don't have to do it like that, but I personally think it looks really good!

Step 2 – You now need to create a free Mailchimp account. You don't need to pay for a membership as you will get your first 2000 contacts for free. That will take a long time to fill up. Make sure you sign up with the same Gmail address that you created in the above step.

Step 3 – You will now need to find a PLR e-book that you can offer as a free e-book. There are many free PLR websites that you can use to find a book. As I said, make sure that the book you are offering is similar to your book title or something that compliments it well.

Step 4 – Once you have found your PLR book. The first step is to create the landing page. To do this, once you have logged into your Mailchimp account now, click on where it says "Campaigns." Then you want to click on where it says "Create a campaign."

You will be taken to a page that looks like this:

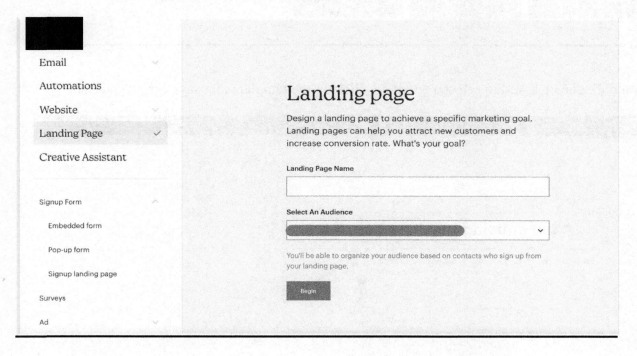

Make sure you select the landing page and select the right audience. You will see a pop-down menu. You should find your author's name + books as the audience. Also, name the landing page something memorable, so you don't get it muddled up with future landing pages. I like to name it as the initials of my book title, this works well for me, and I recommend it to you.

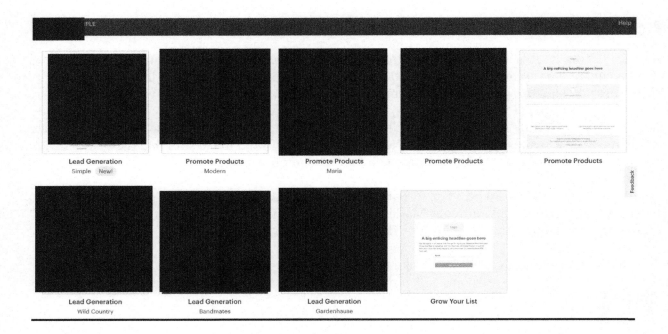

You will then be asked to select a template, click on the template that says "grow your list."

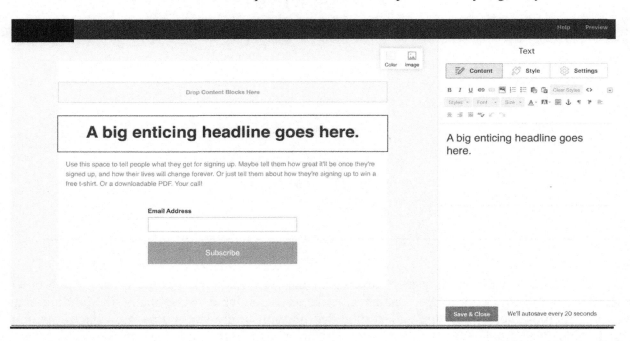

Now it's time to edit the landing page with our own text. You do not have to do it the same as in the example provided above. You can add any writing that you wish. You can also add a background by clicking on where it says "image" Choose a background that is suitable for the theme of the book.

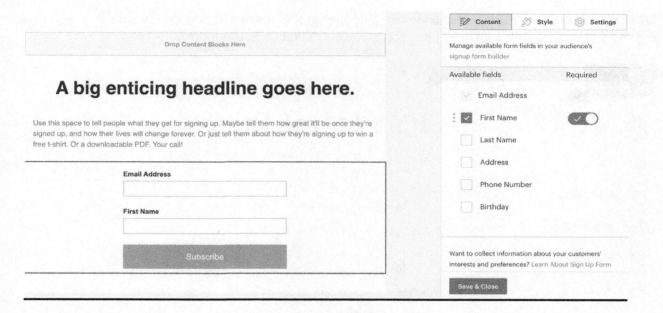

Make sure for the subscribe button that you enable the first name and also the email address of the customer. Make it required. It looks a lot better than just asking for the email address only.

You can mess around with the colors of the button and make it look appealing to you.
Once you have edited the landing page to your liking, click on save & close.

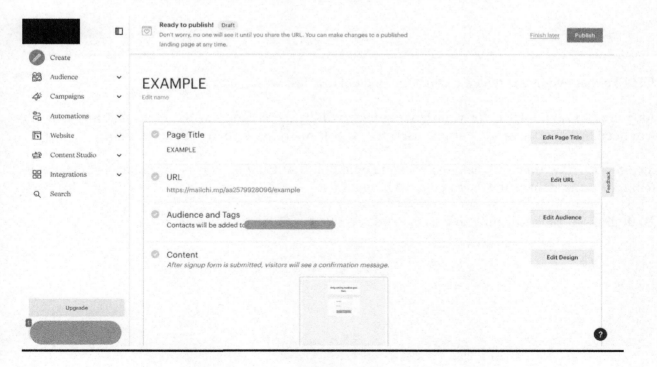

Make sure you check all the details before clicking on the publish button. Make sure the page title and the audience that this landing page for is correct. Then click on publish.

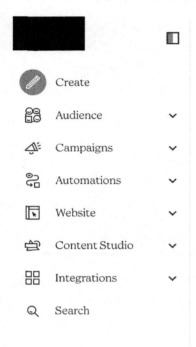

It's a Home Run!

Your landing page is now live on the web.

View your landing page:
https://mailchi.mp/aa2579928096/example

Or share it with your fans:
(f) (y)

Track your campaign stats with the Mailchimp Mobile app. [↗]
Hold your device camera up to the QR code to download.

Just like that, we have created our landing page. How fast was that?

As you can see, the URL for your landing page will be there. Don't worry about that for now. We will need that shortly inside our manuscript in word. As for now, let us move on to the next step.

Step 5 – it's now time to create the backend email on MailChimp. This is the email that customers will receive as soon as they sign up for our email list.

To do this, go back to your home dashboard.

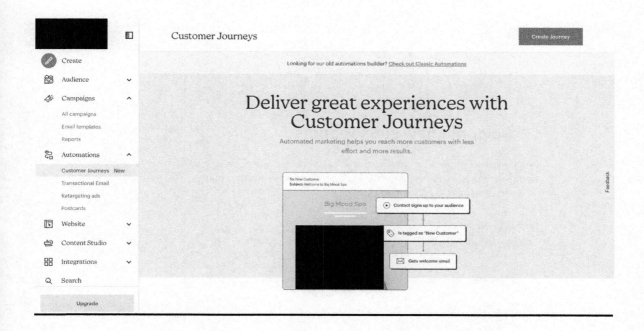

Now go under automations and click on customer journeys. Then click at the top where it says "check out classic automations"

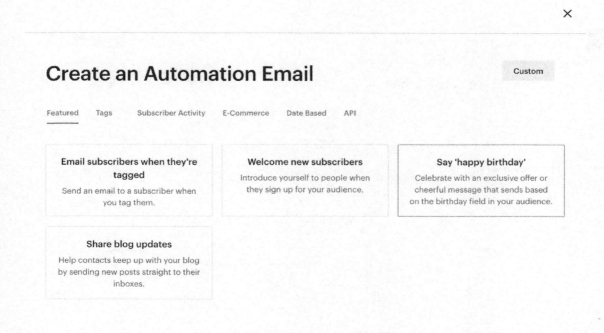

This pop-up will then appear. Click on where it says "Welcome new subscribers."

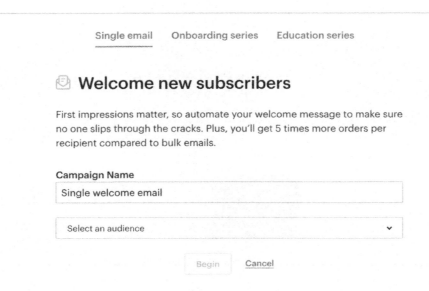

Single email   Onboarding series   Education series

✉ Welcome new subscribers

First impressions matter, so automate your welcome message to make sure no one slips through the cracks. Plus, you'll get 5 times more orders per recipient compared to bulk emails.

Campaign Name

Single welcome email

Select an audience   ⌄

Begin   Cancel

This page will then appear, select the right audience and click on "begin." You can also name your campaign with the initials of the book you are promoting.

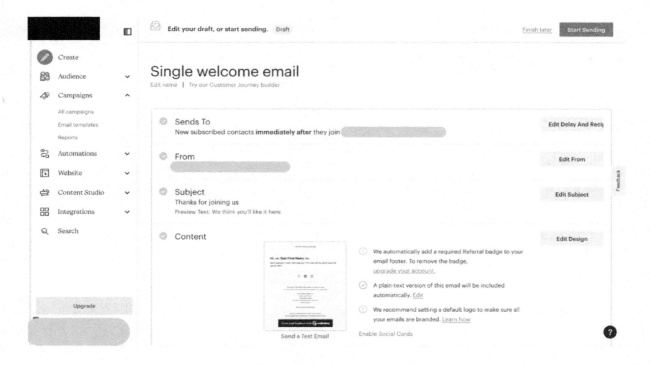

Check these details to make sure they are all correct. Make sure the from email is correct, and the email list is the right one (for e.g., as soon as they join David Richard books).

I would also change the subject line to something else. You can experiment with that. Then click on where it says "Edit design."

It will then ask you to choose a template again. For this one, I go with the "simple text" template.

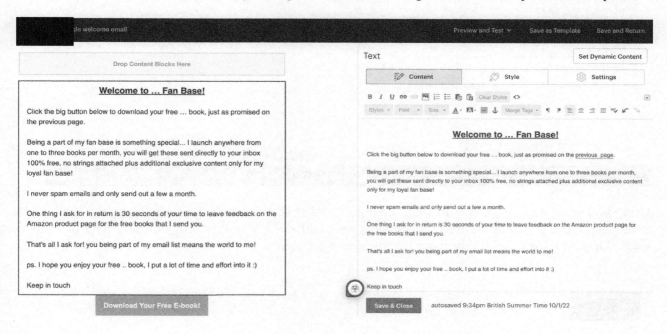

This is the text template that I use for all of my own pen names. Feel free to take it and use it for yourself. You can also come up with your own one. The important thing here is to add the button icon.

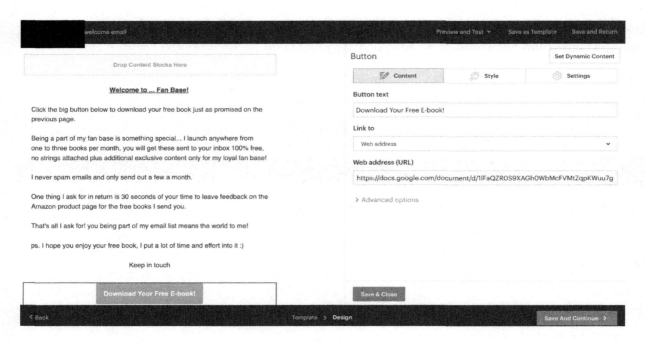

Once you have added the button icon, change the text of the button to something like this. Make sure you select the web address. As for the web address URL, this will be the URL for your e-book. Upload your e-book onto your google drive account.

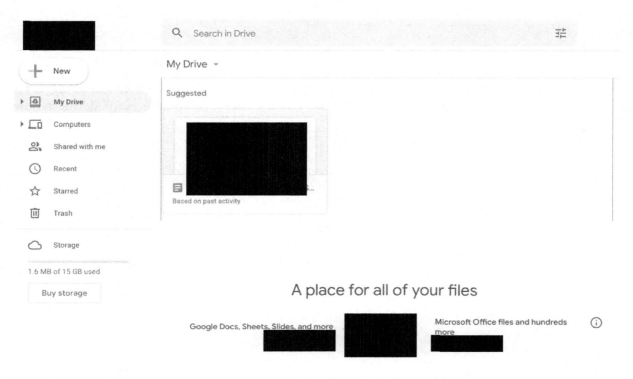

Once you have uploaded your book onto google drive, it will look something like this.

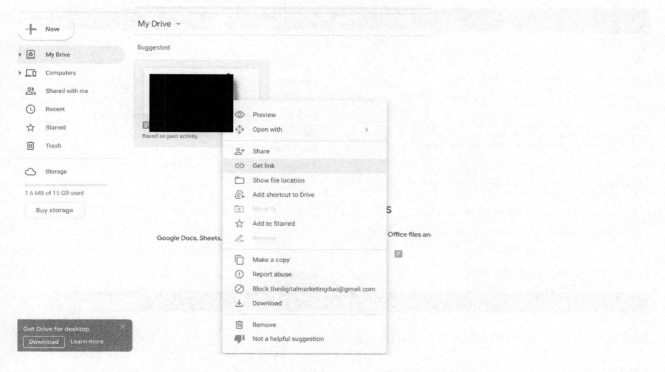

Right-click and click on "get link."

Click on where it says copy link.
Now that we have got the link go back to the other page.

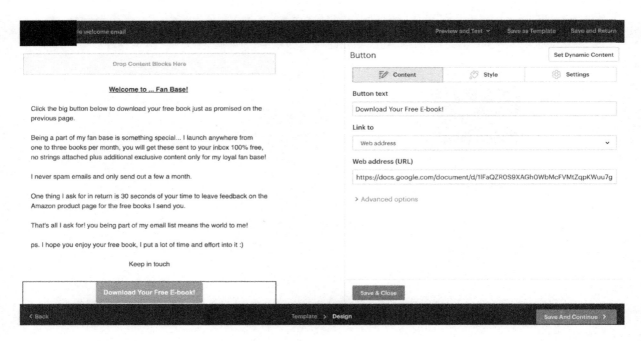

And paste it into the web address (URL) section.

Then click on save & close. Then click on save and continue.

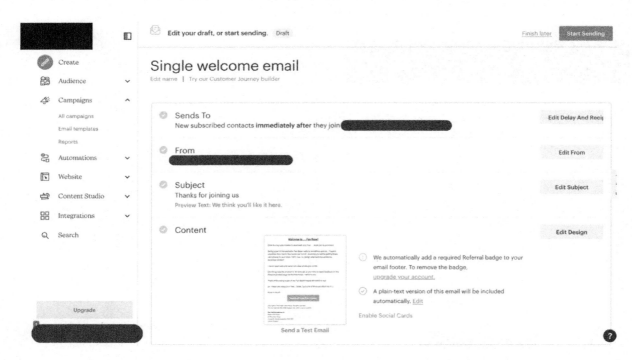

Before you hit the "start sending" button, I always like to send a test email to my personal email address to make sure everything has been set up properly, and the link to the e-book works when you click on it. Once you have confirmed that everything works, click on "start sending."

Now, our only job left is to actually create the funnels. We will use a platform called Canva to do that. Let me show you how to do that now.

Step 5 – Make a free account on canva.com.

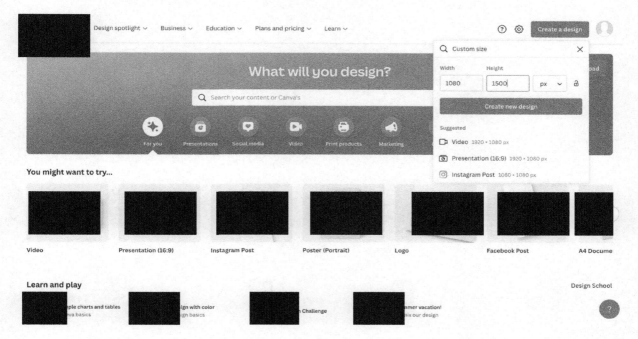

Click on create a design, then click on custom size, copy those dimensions for the width and length.

Let's now firstly create the funnel for the e-book.

You will first need to change your traditional e-book cover to a 3d book cover. To do this, go to a website called www.diybookcovers.com.

Step 1 :

Select the template you want and hit "next."

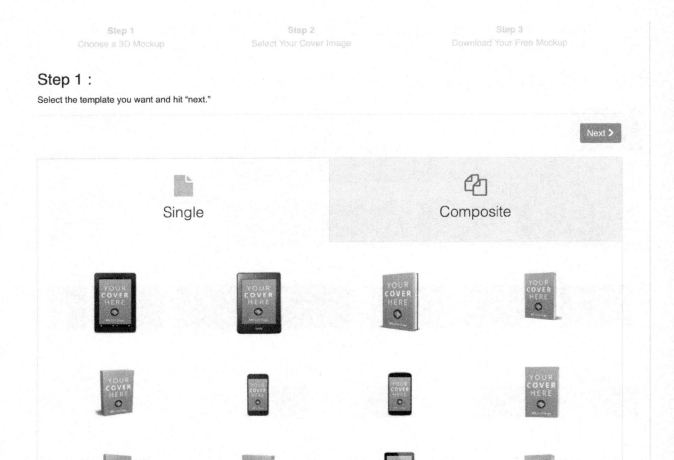

Select any of these, I usually go for the last one on the first row, but you can choose whichever one you want.

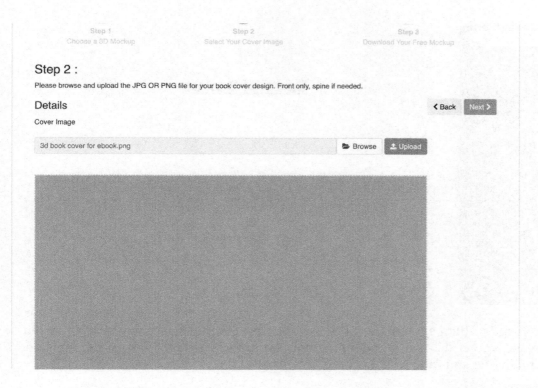

You will then be asked to upload your cover file, upload it and click on next. Then on the next page, click on JPG, not PNG.

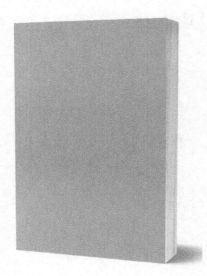

As you can see, I now have a lovely 3d book cover. This one is blank for example purposes. However, your one will be the cover of the free PLR book you are giving away as a bonus.

Now that we have this go back to the Canva page.

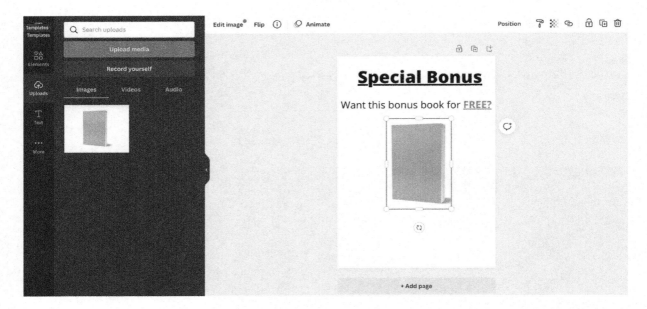

Now upload the image to the page on Canva. It will be on the uploads section, ready for you to drag it into the page. To get the text at the top, simply go to the text and click on the font "add a heading" for the main title and "add a subheading" for the subtitle.

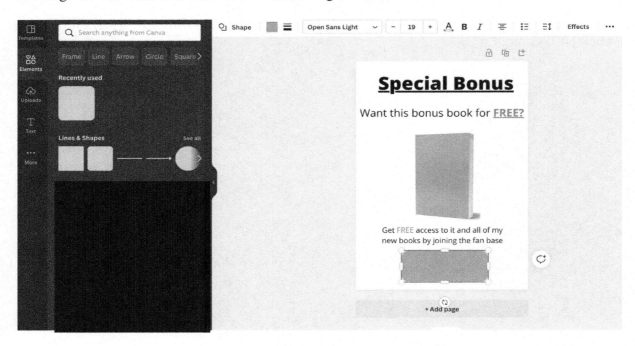

To get the box, go to elements and simply drag it in. You will then drag over the top of it a text box that says something like "click here to join." Make sure you can read what is inside the box, and make the color appropriate.

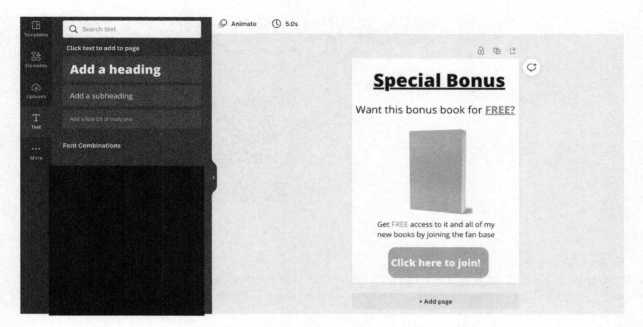

I made it white as that looks appropriate, that is it. We have created the e-book funnel. We will now need to create the same funnel, but for the paperback book.

Everything will be the same apart from the QR code at the bottom.

You will get this QR code by going to a website called https://www.the-qrcode-generator.com/.

You then want to go back to your MailChimp dashboard and copy and paste the URL for the landing page.

This one:

Click on the URL and copy and paste it.

Then go back into the QR code generator and paste it into there.

Paste it into where it says "enter URL," then you want to click on where it says download. Download it to a file on your computer where it will be easy for you to find.

Now you want to go back to Canva and upload it into the uploads section.

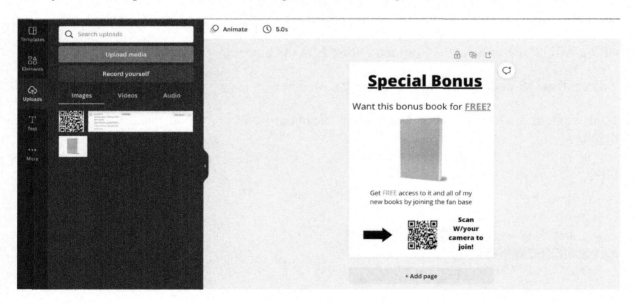

As you can see, it will be on the upload section, simply drag it into Canva, go to the elements tab to get the arrow, and simply add the text on the right-hand side, and we are done!

Now you want to save both of these freebie funnels to your computer. There is only one thing left for us to do.

Step 6 – You will not need to do anything special for the paperback funnel apart from to insert it somewhere at the beginning of your book. Simply drag it from your documents onto your word document file.

However, as for the e-book funnel, we will also need to drag it, but there is an additional step.

Let me show you what I mean.

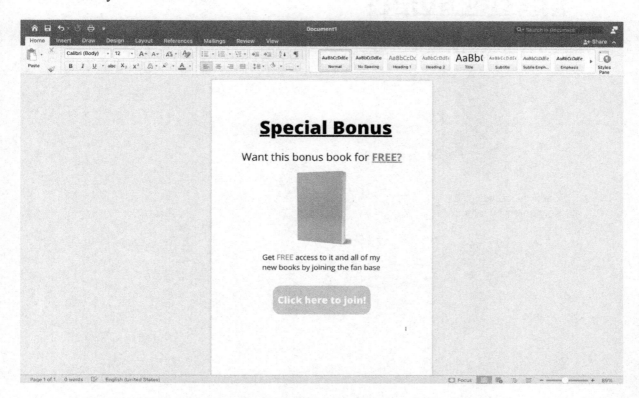

As you can see, I have attached it to my word document, but as of right now, there will be no way for customers to click on the button because we have not set up this functionality yet. To set this up, you want to right-click on the image and click on link.

Special Bonus

Want this bonus book for **FREE?**

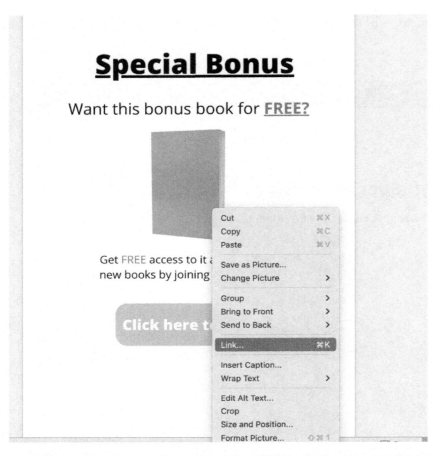

Get the link to your landing page again from your MailChimp dashboard and paste it into the web address tab. Now, when customers are reading your kindle e-book and click on where it says "click here to join," it will take them directly to your landing page, where they can sign up with their email.

That's it! The whole process should not take you longer than 20-30 minutes. It is absolutely vital that you do this with every book. It might grow slowly at first, but once your email list starts to grow, we can really use it to our advantage, and it will save us a lot of time with our arc team.

Chapter 6: Pre-launch Strategy

Up until this point, your book should be ready, cover design ready, you would have hopefully proofread with Grammarly, and your freebie funnel is ready.

There are a few things that we still need to do before we publish our book on KDP.

This is what I like to call a pre-launch strategy. The reason why this strategy is so effective for me is that it allows us to get reviews on our books during the first week when it launches, allowing us to get off to a good start in terms of sales and rankings.

Ideally, we want to aim for around 10/20 reviews on our book within the first week. This is very important because it will serve as great social proof for when we run ads after the first week. Customers like to buy things that already have good reviews, the reviews that we will get within the first few days of launch will help us to build a momentum of early sales and traction. It will also help to convert our amazon ads (I will get onto this in the next chapter).

There are two subscriptions that you need for this strategy to work.

1. **Pubby - https://pubby.co/?invite=11198**
2. Booksprout - **https://booksprout.co**

Let me explain the purpose of each platform to you.

Booksprout

Booksprout is an e-book reading review platform. The purpose of booksprout is for authors to put their e-books on the platform about 10-14 days before the release on Amazon. The platform has thousands of people who like to read and review e-books.

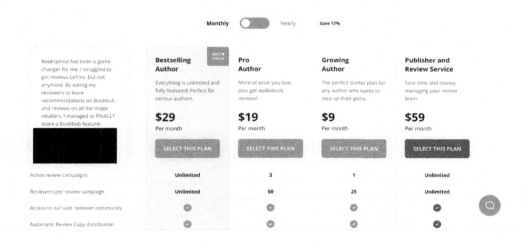

Back when I started publishing a few years ago, booksprout was free. They have recently started charging $9 a month for the subscription, which I still use to this day. I definitely still think it is worth it.

Booksprout allows us to get those 10-15 reviews on Amazon in the first week when we launch. Based on my experience, when I upload a book onto booksprout (Depending on the niche), I usually get around 3-4 people organically picking up my book from their large list of readers. For the rest of them, you have to find people in your niche and offer them your book for free in exchange for a review on amazon once it launches. As you can see, Booksprout offer you 25 reviews per review campaign, before it was 20, which is a nice little increase.

Let me show you how this works.

The first thing you want to do is sign up for the "growing author" subscription for $9 a month. You can sign up with either your personal email address or your pen name Gmail account. Either is fine.

This is what it will look like once you are logged in. What you want to do is click on where it says "pen names." We need to create the author bio before we even upload our book.

Then click on "create new."

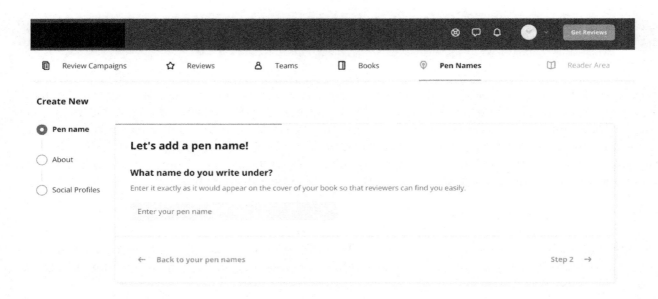

Follow the instructions on this page. It will ask you for the name of the author and the about the author section, and you also have the chance to leave the social profiles for the author (if you have created any for them). I usually leave the social profiles blank.

Once we have created our pen name, we can now upload our books onto booksprout.

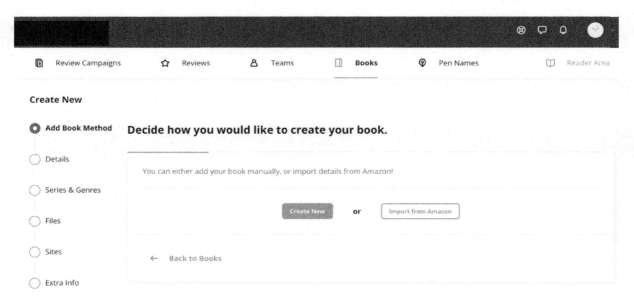

Go to the books tab and click "create new" You will then be taken to a page that looks like this.

We can either import our books directly from amazon or add in the details manually.

Because this is a pre-launch strategy, this would be 10-14 days before our book is even live. Therefore, you would click on "create new".

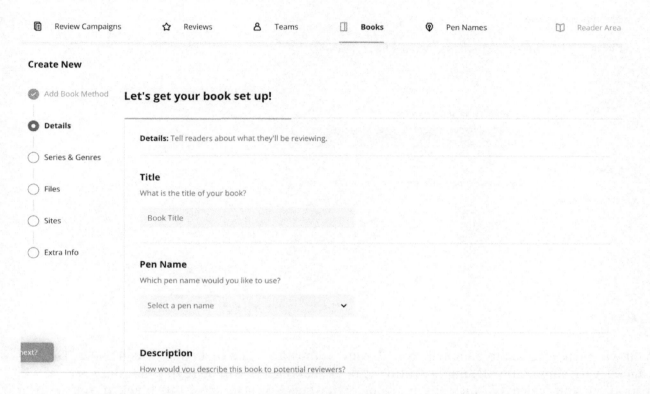

Once you click on create new, you will be asked to fill in some basic information about your book, like the title and subtitle, pen name, book description, and which genre your book belongs to. You will be asked to upload PDF files for your book, etc.

This should not take longer than 5-10 minutes to fill out.

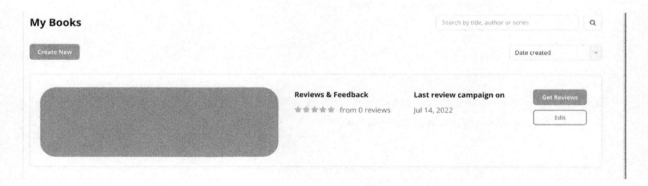

Once you have filled out all of those details, you should find your book under the "my books" section. Note that I have blurred my own book out. However, the title and cover of your book will be there.

Now you will click on where it says "get reviews."

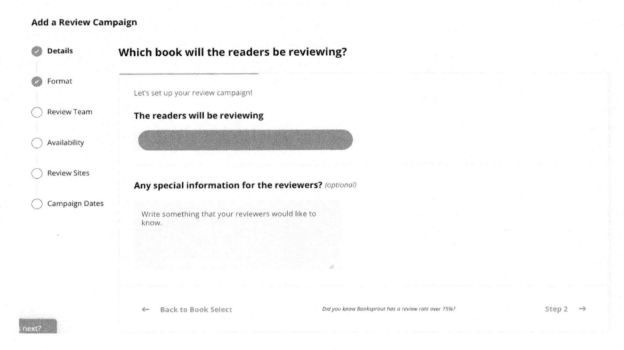

You will then be asked to complete this "Review campaign." The first page, which is the "Details" page, is very simple. It will simply affirm the book that readers will be reviewing. Book sprout will also allow you to leave a message for your reviewers. You can leave this blank if you wish or thank the readers for reading and reviewing your book.

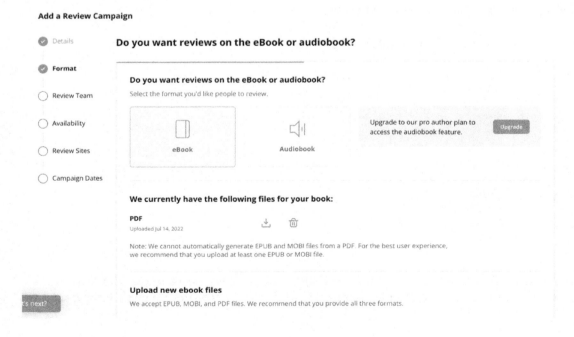

For the "format page," Booksprout will ask if you want the e-book to be reviewed or the Audiobook. Because we are on the $9 membership, we don't have an option to get reviews for the Audiobook. But don't worry! We will get onto reviews for audiobooks in one of the upcoming chapters.

Here is also the page where you can upload the PDF file of your manuscript; if you have not already, do that. Then click on continue.

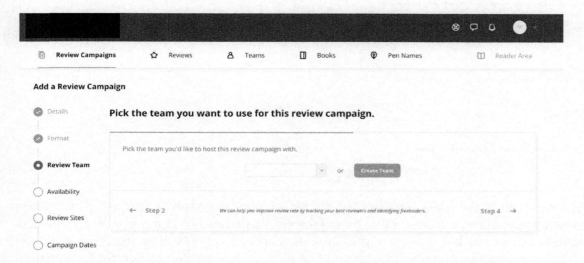

You will then be asked to pick the review team you want to use for this campaign. If you have not set one up already, you can do so quickly under the "Teams tab" you can call it something like "your pen names review team" once you have done that, you can come back here and select the correct review team.

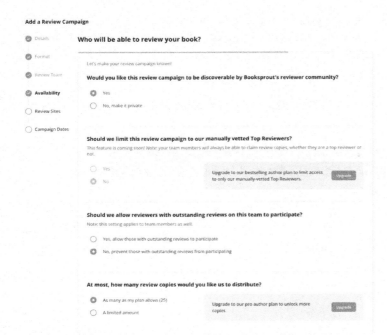

Add a Review Campaign

- Details
- Format
- Review Team
- **Availability**
- Review Sites
- Campaign Dates

Who will be able to review your book?

Let's make your review campaign known!

Would you like this review campaign to be discoverable by Booksprout's reviewer community?

- ○ Yes
- ○ No, make it private

Should we limit this review campaign to our manually vetted Top Reviewers?

This feature is coming soon! Note: your team members will always be able to claim review copies, whether they are a top reviewer or not.

- ○ Yes
- ○ No

Upgrade to our bestselling author plan to limit access to only our manually-vetted Top Reviewers. [Upgrade]

Should we allow reviewers with outstanding reviews on this team to participate?

Note: this setting applies to team members as well.

- ○ Yes, allow those with outstanding reviews to participate
- ○ No, prevent those with outstanding reviews from participating

At most, how many review copies would you like us to distribute?

- ○ As many as my plan allows (25)
- ○ A limited amount

Upgrade to our pro author plan to unlock more copies. [Upgrade]

You will then be taken to the "Availability" tab. In this section, Booksprout will ask if we would like our review campaign to be discoverable by Booksprout's reviewer community. We will select yes to this question. For the last question, you have the choice to choose how many reviews you would like for this campaign. Remember that you can have 25 review copies per book campaign. You can decide to go with as many as you want. However, if you want more than 25 reviews for each book you upload on booksprout, you will have to update your membership. 25 is fine, and I usually stick to this.

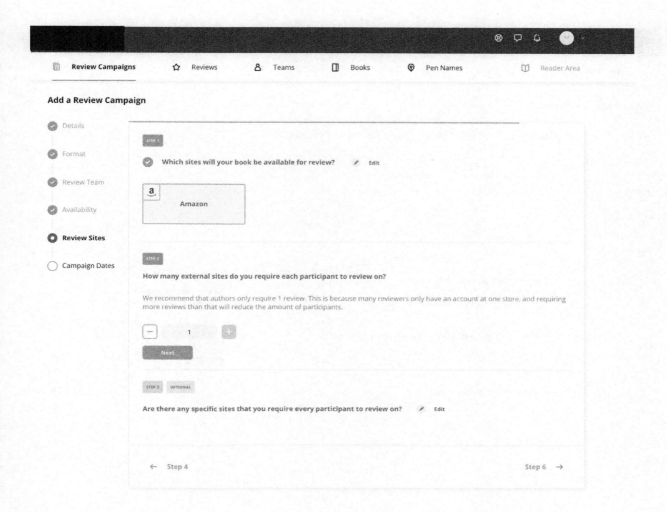

The next page is the review sites page. Booksprout will simply ask us which sites our books will be available for review. Make sure you select amazon for this option. You will then be asked if there are any specific sites that you require every participant to review. I usually leave this blank, as amazon is sufficient for us.

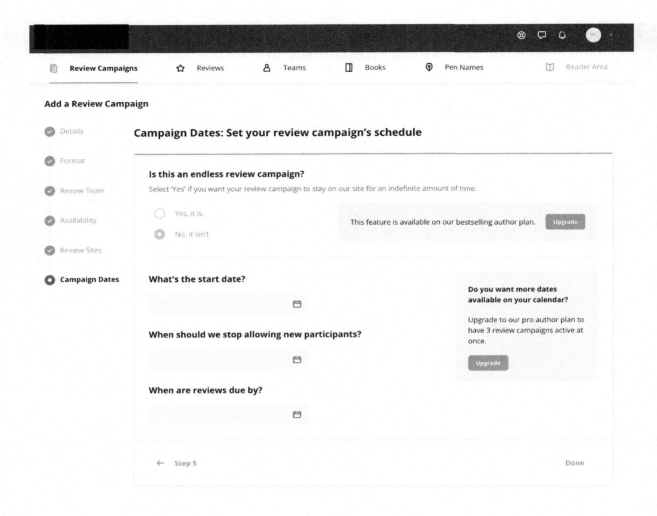

The last page is the campaign dates, this page is very important, and you need to make sure that you do this correctly.

The start date is the date that you upload your book onto Booksprout and the date that you start seeking pre-readers to read your book and review it when it becomes live on amazon.

I would recommend that you set the date that Booksprout stops allowing new participants to pick up your book arc at least five days from when you plan to launch it on amazon. You don't want to leave it too close to your release date on Amazon, as readers will not have enough time to read your book and leave a review when you launch.

The review due date should be the date that you plan to launch on Amazon.

Now we have created our review campaign. It is active. You should expect around 3-5 people to organically pick up a copy of your book, read and review it.

It is now your job to find the rest of those 25 reviewers. This is the manual part of this strategy that may take a few hours. This is why I stress the importance of building your own email list because when you gradually build up your email list, you will not have to do this again for future book launches.

Click on the "share" button on the side of the review campaign.

It will open up this pop-up:

This is your arc link for your book. This is the link that you will distribute to potential readers. Once they click on the link, they will be able to pick up your book and read it.

Let's now discuss how you can find the remaining participants to read your book pre-launch.

Like I have already said, at the start, this will feel like hard work, but you have to push through. It might take a few days, but it will surely be worth it in the end.

The best way to find interested readers, based on my experience, is to go into Facebook groups and Reddit groups of your niche.

For example, if you have created a book on affiliate marketing, you would go into affiliate marketing groups on Facebook and Reddit. Make sure you read the group rules, as some groups do not allow promotion posts to be posted.

Once you have verified that it is okay for you to promote your book on these groups, you want to create a post that reads something like:

"Hi guys!

I have written a book on ... and I am currently looking for a group of pre-readers to read my book for free in exchange for a review on amazon when I launch in the next 10/14 days.
If you are interested in my book, please reach out via dm."

Something as simple as this works really well for me. You do not need to overcomplicate things. Post this message in as many groups related to your niche as you can. Wait a few hours for your posts to get some interactions. Once people reply to you with interest in your book, you will message them privately.

Before you send them your ARC link, it is important to make sure:

- That they have an amazon.com account that has spent at least $50, the reason why this is a must is that as per Amazon's guidelines, you need to have spent at least $50 to be able to leave a review. This is something that I was not aware of previously, and it ended up biting me in the foot because I had a lot of readers that wanted to leave reviews but simply couldn't.

- Make sure they are in the US, so their review is visible on amazon.com, not any other amazon marketplace. This is very important! You may find readers with amazon accounts outside of the US. This is a problem because, at first, we want to focus on gathering reviews for the US amazon book marketplace as it is the largest and will generate the most book sales. After we have more than 20-30 reviews on amazon.com, you can find reviewers from other countries to leave you reviews for the same book but on a different amazon marketplace.

That is pretty much it. When the date arrives when your book becomes live on amazon, they will get an email reminder by Booksprout to leave their review. The good thing about Booksprout is that you actually get the reader's personal email address as well once they sign up for your arc, meaning that if they don't leave it on the first day, you can follow up with them by email in the next following days after that.

Now that we have got Booksprout out the way let's talk about Pubby.

Pre-launch promo sites

There are also some pre-launch promo sites that you can use to get off to a good start for when you launch your book. These are essentially websites that have huge email lists of readers in various niches.

What you would need to do is reach out to a few promo sites about 2-3 weeks from when you plan to launch and book a slot with them for when you launch on day 1. They will then promote your book to their email list on the day you launch, and it will give you a huge boost.

When you publish your book on Amazon, the first 30 days of launch is what I like to call the incubation period. This is the period when amazon would like to see if your book will be a great seller or not. This also means that during this period, they will rank your book a lot higher and give it priority over others. If you show amazon during the first 30 days that you can get a nice consistent stream of sales, they will most likely maintain your ranking positions for your keywords after that period. These promo sites help with just that because it puts lots of eyeballs on your book when it just launches.

Some great pre-launch promo sites that I have experience with are:

• Bargain booksy.
• Bknights on Fiverr.

They are both very affordable and can make a huge difference, so I would definitely recommend that you give them both a try and see what works well for you.

Pubby

Pubby is a platform where you read other people's books. For each book that you read, you earn something called "snaps," you then use those snaps to get reviews on your own books. This does not go against Amazon's TOS for reviews because we don't know the authors personally or their books. Therefore, we are not directly exchanging reviews with other authors.

Pubby has two pricing strategies, and they also offer a free ten-day trial, which gives you more than enough time to see if the platform will be of use to you.

The two plans that Pubby offers are:

- $17.99 monthly for up to 10 books – This is the plan that will suffice you for the first few months. If you publish two books a month, you will be able to have this plan for the first five months. You may then need to upgrade.

- $29.99 monthly for an unlimited number of books – After you have exceeded the ten books limit, then it would make sense to go for this plan.

Let me explain how Pubby works.

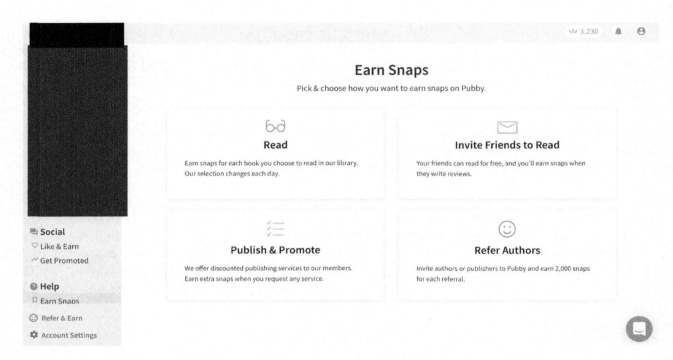

This is what the dashboard will look like when you first sign up. The first thing that you should do is add your book. If you scroll up a bit on the left-hand side, you will see a button for you to add your book. You will be asked to fill out a few details like your book title, author, a description of your book, etc. It's similar to Booksprout.

There are a few different ways you can earn snaps on Pubby.

Invite friends to read – you can invite friends to the Pubby platform, and in exchange, you will receive snaps. They have not made it clear how much, but it is certainly an option for you.

Publishing & promote – Pubby also offers a variety of publishing services like book description, ad copy, etc. If you order one of these services from Pubby, you get snaps for that as well. I have personally not tried any of these services myself, so I can't recommend them to you.

Refer authors – if you refer other authors to the Pubby platform, you will get 2000 snaps, which can get you about two reviews for your book.

Read – This is the most common way to earn snaps on the platform. When you click on read, you will have the following options below to choose from. When you sign up with Pubby, you have the option to either list your book for a free read, meaning that anybody can pick it up with their snaps for free, or a kindle unlimited read, meaning they need to have a kindle unlimited account and read your book through there, or outright purchase your book. To offer your book for a verified purchase, you need to pay a one-off $15 dollar fee. Once that is paid, you will be able to list your books for purchase.

📖 Free	ku Kindle Unlimited	✓ Verified Purchase	🏍 Quick Read	👏 Most Snaps
🎯 Business	☕ Self Help	🥑 Health	🔍 Mystery	🍰 Romance

This is fantastic, and if you really think about it, we could very easily make back our money every month solely based on the verified purchases we get for our book through the Pubby platform. Not only that, but you are also receiving a verified review on amazon.

Let me explain the difference between a verified review and an unverified review.

⭐⭐⭐⭐⭐ **Informative and balanced**

Reviewed in the United States on May 14, 2022

Verified Purchase

This was not a pump and dump where the author wanted us all to buy bitcoin and then sell his, but is a wide ranging, balanced view of digital assets. He covered the technology, the bitcoin network, investing in digital assets, NFTs, and getting started. Pretty much everything you need to know to get your foot in the digital asset door. I like that he covered some of the downsides of digital assets as well as the upsides. I particularly liked he only recommended investing 1% of your net worth in digital assets. This felt like a reasonable amount given the volatility in the digital asset space. I personally still worry about things like regulation and losing my encryption keys (and therefore the whole asset), but author does a good job explaining those risks and how to mitigate somewhat. I will never understand the value of NFTs but that is probably just me.

5 people found this helpful

This is a verified review. As you can see, it has the "verified purchase" badge at the top of the review.

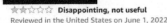

★★☆☆☆ **Disappointing, not useful**

Reviewed in the United States on June 1, 2022

I was really disappointed in this book. I'm already convinced that I need a portion of my portfolio in digital assets, and I wanted this book to help me understand how to do that. It didn't. Half of the book is nothing but totally worthless lists of various organizations and companies associated with digital assets, with zero information as to which I should use, or why. The rest of the book convinced me that the regulatory picture and investment vehicles for digital assets are no where close to being ready for a routine investor with a managed portfolio in an established financial planning firm. I was left more confused and more frustrated than I was when I started the book, and more convinced than ever that digital assets are not ready for prime time investing. Give me a digital assets index ETF available in mainstream brokerage accounts like Schwab, and then maybe I'll be ready to commit a portion of my portfolio to digital assets. But if I have to set up a separate account, maintain a digital wallet and personally safeguard a key that if lost wipes out the entire investment, track and manage all of my records manually for tax reporting, and negotiate a regulatory minefield of unclear tax and reporting implications, no thanks. I have relied on Ric Edelman for years for the most clear and objective investment advice available, but his big push to get people to invest now in crypto seems inconsistent with his past advice.

3 people found this helpful

Helpful | Report abuse

This is an example of an unverified review. As you can see, it does not have the "verified purchase" badge at the top of the review. Unverified reviews are not bad. I have a lot of them; however, the verified reviews are always a lot more valuable because it serves as better social proof, and when a review is verified, it will appear on other amazon marketplaces for our books as well for, e.g., the UK, Germany, Italian, etc. This is super valuable to us because it will help us to generate sales for the book on those marketplaces as well as in the US. Therefore, you should always aim for verified purchase reviews.

As you can see, you can also choose the niche in which you want to read other authors' books in. Just as you have the option to list your book for a verified purchase, so do other authors, and even though you would have to buy that author's book to review it, you receive double the number of snaps, meaning that you can then get double the number of reviews for your own book later on.

Once your book has been approved by Pubby (this will usually take a few hours), and you have built up some snaps, you can get your book reviewed.

CHOOSE YOUR REVIEW OPTIONS

Turnaround Time

(3)—(2)—(1) DAYS

Choose the number of days your reader is given to read your book
and turn in their review.

The recommended days based on your page length: 3 days.

☐ **Recommended Reader**   ↙ 150

We'll find a reader who is likely to enjoy your book based
on their reading history. It may take longer to find a reader.

Total: ↙ 1110

Pubby also has a few more options that are very helpful. They allow you to choose the turnaround time that you want your book to be reviewed. During the launch, you want as many reviews as you can in the first week, so I tend to go for either 1 or 2 days. You also have the option of recommending your book to a reader who is likely to enjoy your book based on their reading history, which is very helpful as they will most likely leave a positive review of your book.

Once you click on "get reviewed," it usually takes a few hours for your book to be picked up, so it is a lot quicker than doing the manual work for Booksprout. With that said, I recommend you do both so you can get the greatest number of reviews on your book during the launch.

Overall Pubby is a very helpful tool, and I would definitely recommend it. You can very easily get 100+ reviews on your book with just Pubby alone if you play the long game.

Your pricing strategy

How you price your e-books and paperbacks will be largely dependent on your competitor's prices, you want to make your prices competitive so you can continue to make sales. When you just launch, though, it's a good idea to price your book a bit lower than your competitors. I do this for the first 30 days so that I can get the greatest number of purchases possible and so that I can rank my book on the amazon first page.

For example, if the best sellers on the first page price their book at $4.99 for the e-book and $12.95 for the paperback, I will price my e-book at $2.99 and my paperback at $9.99 for the first month. After that, I will raise the price of my book again and continue to run my amazon ads (more on this in the next chapter).

Kindle select

Kindle Select is a program that amazon specifically created for authors and publishers who publish on KDP. You have the option to enrol your e-book into Kindle select on the last page when you are drafting your e-book. The benefit of being on kindle select is that you get five days where you can promote your book for free, meaning that people can download your book for free during this period. Again, this is a very good idea because the more e-book downloads you get, the more it will help with your ranking.

Another benefit of joining the kindle select program is that your book will be available on kindle unlimited. There are over a million subscribers on the kindle unlimited program. Your book will be made available for readers on that program, and you will get paid for each page read from your book. Although it is little, it is still a nice bit of extra income, and it can certainly add up at the end of every month if you have a few books.

I would say the default should always be that you are to opt-in for the kindle select. You should leave your book in the program for at least 6-12 months. During this time, you want to monitor your sales for that book. If they continue well, keep your book in kindle select. If they don't, you can always take it out of kindle select and upload your book onto other aggregator websites such as Ingramspark, draft2digital, google books, etc.

When you sign up with kindle select, you agree to amazons' terms that say that you are not allowed to distribute your e-book outside of the Amazon kindle store. I do just want to clarify that this is only for e-books and not relevant for paperbacks.

This is why I believe you should leave your book on kindle select for at least 6-12 months because the majority of readers will be on kindle. However, if you are not happy with the number of sales after that time, ask KDP to remove you from the kindle select program and upload your e-book on other aggregators as well.

I have had some books that did not do so well on kindle select. The moment I took them out of kindle select and listed them on draft2digital, Ingramspark, and google books, the sale numbers quickly shot up. It's a matter of testing and seeing what works well for you.

Chapter 7: Amazon AMS Ads

Amazon ads are the bloodline for our publishing business, and you will need to keep them running if you want to make a stable stream of revenue from your books.

Before we get into the technicalities of amazon ads, there are a few things that you will need to understand.

AMS ads work on a bidding system.

That means that you will set how much you want to bid for a specific keyword.

When someone then searches for a keyword that you are bidding on, the most **relevant** book that is bidding on that keyword will show first in the rankings.

But why the one that is most relevant and not the highest bidder, you may ask?

Let me give you an example.

Even though book A might have a higher bid on the keyword "Stock market" ($0.75) compared to book B ($0.65), Amazon may still favor book b because:

• It is of higher quality.
• Amazon thinks it will convert better and get more sales.
• Amazon thinks the book is more relevant to your customer's search intent.

This is very important to understand because it then shows us the importance of producing a high-quality book that our readers will enjoy.

There are a few metrics that you need to know related to amazon ads. Let's go through them.

Budget – This is the campaign budget that you will set up.

• Impressions – How many people your ad is put Infront of.

• Clicks – How many clicks your amazon ads are getting.

• CTR – How often a customer decides to click on your ad when it is put in front of them (clicks/ impressions).

• CPC – This is the average cost you are paying per bid when somebody clicks on your ad.

• Orders – This is the number of orders placed. Note that they can be behind sometimes by 12 hours.

• ACOS – Average costs of sales. This is calculated by dividing the total spend by your attributed sales, then multiplied by 100.
For e.g., if you spend $20 on ads and get $100 back in sales in return, your ACOS will be 20%

Generally speaking, we are aiming for an ACOS that is below 30% for the ad campaign to be profitable. However, this does also depend on the price of your paperback or e-book.

A final thing to consider is that Amazon ads will only show you your sales and not the total royalties that you take home.

The total royalties per sale are usually 40%-50% of what each sale shows up as on the dashboard.

For e.g., if your campaign is showing $3000 in sales, you should expect to take home anywhere between $1200-$1500.

Subtract your ad spend from that $1200 - $1500, and you have your profit.

Another final thing to consider is that the amazon ads dashboard will show only your sales through ads and not any organic sales. They will come through the reports section on KDP.

Targetwords for ads

Targetwords are essentially keywords, but not the same keywords for our book topics. Instead, they are keywords for AMS ads.

These 'targetwords' are used to target our customers in the campaign. As you can imagine, Amazon has millions of customers, so we need to be able to target the right ones. These targetwords allow us to target the right audience for our campaign, which is crucial to having a profitable campaign.

There will be three main methods that we will use to gather targetwords:

- Method #1 – The first page results for that keyword
- Method #2 – Through the Publisher Rocket tool
- Method #3 – Through the Amazon search bar

Now that we know the three methods of collecting targetwords let's discuss the type of targetwords that we will be collecting

1. " Search targetwords" – for this. We will generate 300 – 500 targetwords
2. " Author targetwords" – for this, we will also generate 300– 500 targetwords
3. "ASIN targetwords" – we will generate around 100 targetwords for these

So, we will be using the Amazon search bar, the first page results, and Publisher rocket to find these targetwords.

Search targetwords

Example book – Investing in the stock market

You will then search in the Amazon search bar – "Investing" &" stock market." The suggested results are our first set of targetwords. This is the Amazon search bar method. Simply type them in, and copy the suggested titles by Amazon.

Copy them into something that looks like this. Put them in the first column, that is, the search targetwords.

Search Targetwords (method 1, 2 and 3)	Author Targetwords (method 1 & 2)	ASIN Targetwords (method 2)

We will then do the first-page results method. So, we will search this time "Investing in the stock market" and take the book titles on the first and second page and copy them again in our excel spreadsheet.

Finally, we will go to publisher rocket and again search "investing" &" stock market" in the AMS keyword search tool. This is the first time mentioning this tool. Publisher rocket is a one-off $99 tool; however, this tool is very important for your publishing business, and you will use it frequently.

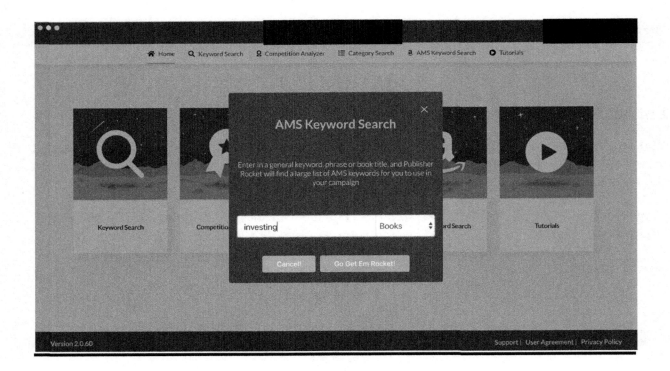

Once you are on publisher rocket, click on the AMS keyword search tool and type in the relevant terms. Then click on "go get 'em rocket."

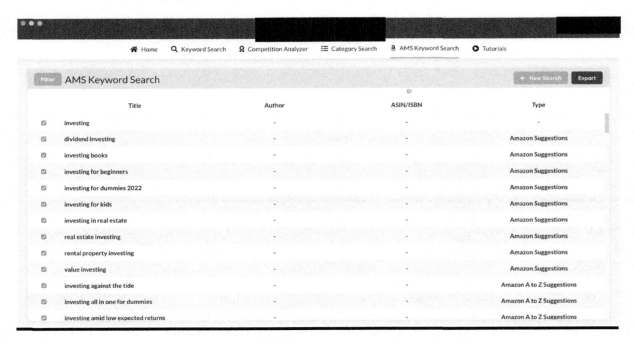

It will then display a large list of keywords relevant to our search. Export this file to a file on your computer. You want to search for at least 3-4 different variants for the publisher rocket method. This will allow us to reach about 300 search targetwords. For e.g., you could search for variations like "Investing for beginners," "the stock market for beginners," "Investing in stocks for beginners," etc. Make sure you export them and store them in a memorable file on your computer.

The next type of targetwords are ASIN targetwords

We will only be using the publisher rocket method to generate these.
ASINS (Amazon standard identification number) is how amazon identifies items and differentiates them from other products.

We can place our book ads onto similar products by targeting their ASIN numbers.

With ASIN targetwords, because the exported file from the search targetwords already has these, we do not need to export them again.

Simply go to your exported file, copy the ASINS and paste them into the ASINS target words on the excel spreadsheet.

Let's move on to the last type of targetwords, author targetwords

Author targetwords

To get these target words, we will only be using the publisher rocket method and the first page results on amazon.

Author target words are basically the author names of the top competitors in the keyword that you are trying to rank for.

Again, we would be searching "investing in the stock market" and taking the author's names on the first and second pages.

As for the publisher rocket method for author targetwords, then the exported file for the search targetwords will also already have the author names on there. Therefore, you do not need to search them all again and export them again on publisher rocket. Simply copy and paste them into the author targetwords section on the excel spreadsheet.

At this stage, the three columns on your excel spreadsheet should be filled in with search targetwords, ASIN targetwords, and author targetwords. There is still one more thing we have to do before we take these to the advertising dashboard.

Open up a google sheets page and copy one column in at a time in section A.

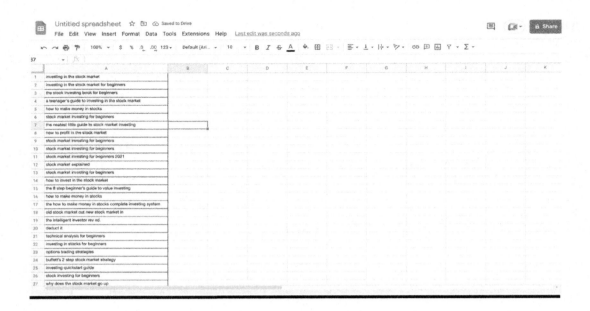

The above is an example of our search targetwords, but you will be doing this with all of them.

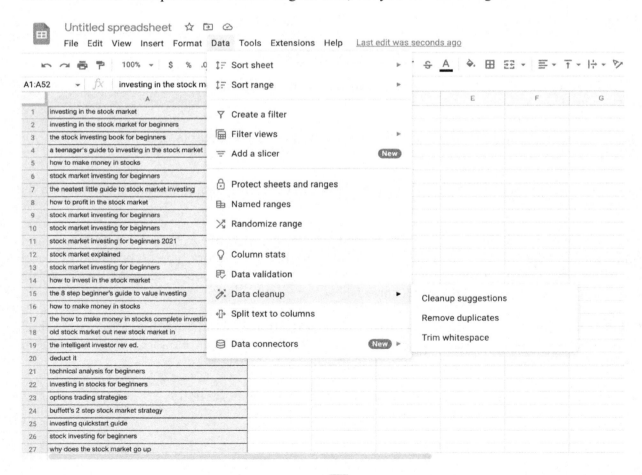

Once you have copied them inside, highlight all of the targetwords in column a, go to the "data" tab, hover over data clean-up, and click on remove duplicates. What this will do is remove any duplicate targetwords that we have, as we don't want to enter the same ones into amazon ads.

Do this for all three types of targetwords, then re-copy them back into the excel spreadsheet.

Now it's time to start running your ads. The question is, how do you get to the ads dashboard?

Once you are inside your KDP account, click on the marketing tab.

You will then be taken to a page that looks like this.

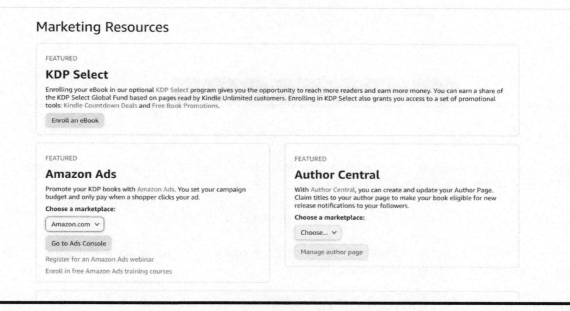

Make sure you select the amazon.com marketplace, then click on go to ads console.

You may first be asked to insert a payment method, do that before moving on. One thing to note with AMS ads is that you get charged once you reach a specific threshold of ad spend, unlike with PPC ads with Amazon FBA, where your ad spend gets deducted from your sales. This is important to know because it means you will have to manage your capital carefully throughout the month to ensure that you will have enough to keep your ads running throughout the whole month.

Once you have added your payment method, you will be taken to a page that looks like this.

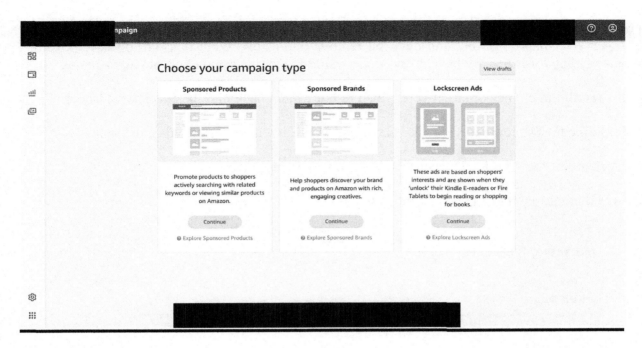

Now before I show you how to set up your ads, there are some things that you need to know.

Once we get into the amazon ads platform, we will create eight different types of campaigns (or you can do four if you are strapped for cash).

Four will target your e-book, and the other four will target your paperback.

So, in total, it will be eight campaigns consisting of pairs that are exactly the same, just one targeting e-book and the other a paperback.

The campaign types that we will run are:

1) Manual targeting campaign – these will include the search targetwords and author targetwords we gathered before.

2) ASIN targeting campaign (x2 – two types) – this type of campaign will place your books below other books on their product pages.

3) Automatic campaign – this is an automatically generated campaign by Amazon, mainly used to find out which targetwords work and which don't.

This is what a manual campaign will look like in the eyes of the customer.

This is what an ASIN campaign will look like in the eyes of the customer.

How Amazon Ads Work

Amazon ads have three main levels that you need to know:

- Level one – Portfolios – this is basically a folder where we organize our different campaigns. Within those campaigns, we obviously have our targetwords that we have curated.
- Level two – Campaigns – This is where we have the actual campaigns.
- Level three – Targetwords – This is where the targetwords are located.

Let me break this down for you further with an illustration

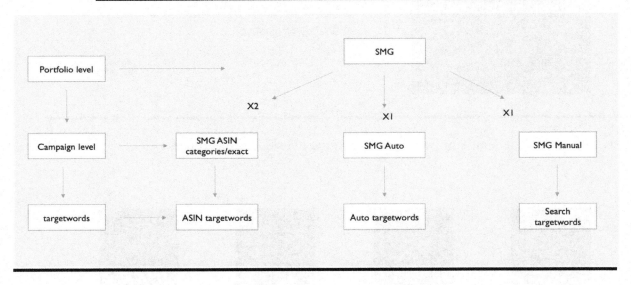

As you can see, at the top level, we have the portfolio level. The example, in this case, is SMG, which is an acronym for your book title. In this case, it would be "stock market for beginners."

In the portfolio section, we have to create the portfolio file with the acronym of your book. The reason why we do this for all of our books is to keep a bit of organization. If we had all of our ads in one folder or portfolio, you can imagine how hectic it would be. It would also be difficult to analyze the ads and see where we can improve.

Campaign level

At the campaign level, I like to name my campaigns by using the acronym (SMG), then putting a dash and explaining what type of campaign it is. That could be:

- SMG – Auto
- SMG – Manual
- SMG – ASIN categories/ ASIN Exact

Targetwords level

Once we create the campaigns, we now have to add the targetwords.

These are the targetwords that you will bid on, and this is the place where we place our starting bids for each of these targetwords.
We will add custom text (short) that will hopefully catch the attention of our intended buyers.

Amazon may suggest even more targetwords. I will show you how to do this properly.

When you now see the above illustration of what this looks like, it will make a lot of sense to you.

Let's now take you through the first step, which is creating a portfolio for the book that you want to advertise.

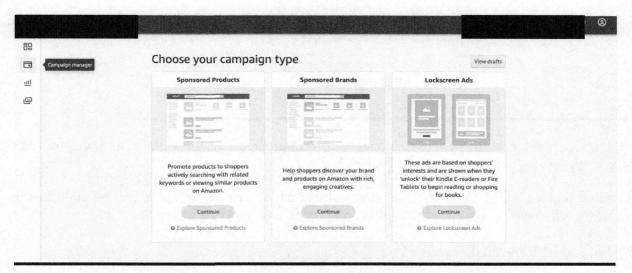

To do this, you will click on campaign manager, as shown above in the image.

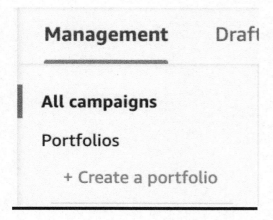

Your dashboard will be empty as you have not run any ads before. However, you should see this on the left-hand side. You want to click on "Create a portfolio," then type in the acronym of your book and create a fresh portfolio.

For example, if your book title was Cryptocurrency for beginners, you should call your portfolio "CFB."

Now it should look something like this once you have created your portfolio. The portfolio right now is empty, so let's start creating our first ad.

Remember that we will be creating four types of campaigns. However, there will be eight ads in total, as we will have to copy what we do for our e-book also for the paperback.

Click on "Create Campaign."

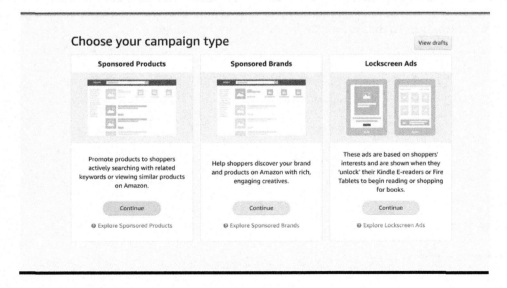

Now you want to click on the "sponsored products" campaign, click on continue.

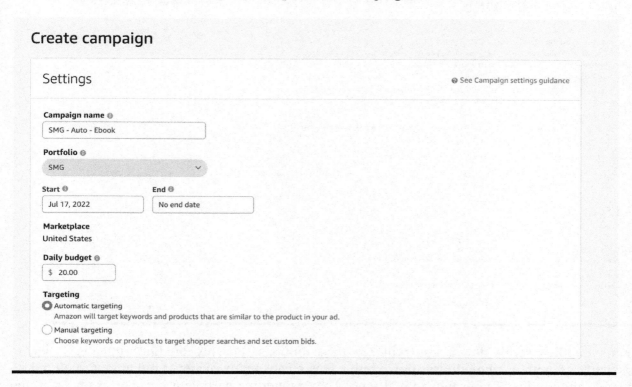

Notice how I name my campaigns. I start off with the portfolio name, which is SMG. I then insert a dash, then "auto," meaning that this is an auto campaign, and lastly, I put in "e-book," showing that this is the auto campaign for my e-book. Doing things like this at your campaign level Is very good as it makes it easier to read and remember and also later to analyze your ads. Make sure you also select the correct portfolio in the dropdown menu. When you are just starting out, you will only have one portfolio. However, as you add more books, you will need to become mindful of selecting the correct portfolio.

The next stage will be deciding your daily budget. I usually start off at $20 a day. If you are on a budget, you can start at $15 a day. I usually find that the Amazon ads will never really spend the full amount on a daily basis anyway. It will most likely spend 75% of your daily budget. $20 is a good amount to start with as it guarantees that we will get impressions on our ads, which is very important, of course.

If we start off with a very low budget, Amazon will not be able to show our ads to a lot of people due to the limited number of impressions you can get with such a low budget.

Make sure you select automatic targeting for the auto ad.

Campaign bidding strategy ⓘ

❷ Choose your bidding strategy

◉ **Dynamic bids - down only**
We'll lower your bids in real time when your ad may be less likely to convert to a sale. Any campaign created before April 22, 2019 used this setting.

◯ **Dynamic bids - up and down** ⓘ
We'll raise your bids (by a maximum of 100%) in real time when your ad may be more likely to convert to a sale, and lower your bids when less likely to convert to a sale.

◯ **Fixed bids**
We'll use your exact bid and any manual adjustments you set, and won't change your bids based on likelihood of a sale.

⌄ Adjust bids by placement (replaces Bid+) ⓘ

Ad Format

❷ Choosing your ad format

◉ **Custom text ad**
Add custom text to your ad to give customers a glimpse of the book.

◯ **Standard ad**
Choose this option to advertise your products without custom text.

When you then scroll down, you will see these options. For my bidding strategy, I like to personally go with dynamic bids – down only. This means that whichever bid amount you put in, amazon can only lower your bids in real-time. They cannot increase your bid. For example, if you bid $0.30 for the targetword "Investing for beginners," Amazon cannot charge you anything more than that.

If you go with dynamic bids – up and down, the bids can be raised in real-time, so even though you originally might have bidded $0.30 for a targetword, Amazon could end up doubling the cost of that bid due to maybe the intensified competition in that keyword. Therefore, I like to always go with dynamic bids down only. It works well with me, and it should definitely work well with you as well.

In terms of the ad format, you can either opt for the custom text ad or the standard ad. The custom text ad means that you have some text side by side with your ad while it is being displayed, while the standard ad is just the ad without any text. I personally go for the standard ad, but you can go with the custom text ad if you have some interesting hooks in mind that will hook the customer's attention. One thing to note, though, is that you have to be very careful with what you put in the custom text ad, as amazon will not accept everything. You can have a read on their guidelines for a custom text add-on KDP.

Once we scroll down, it will now be time to add your book.

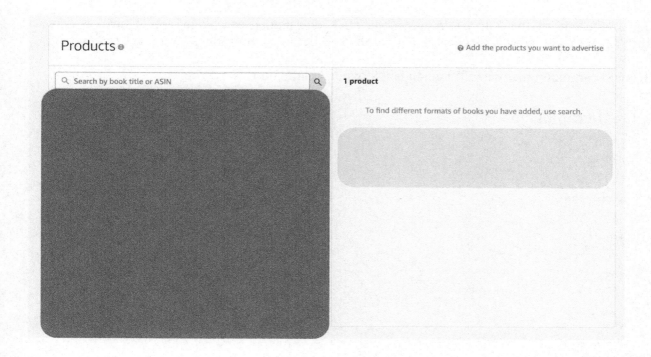

Make sure to select your ebook first (or whichever one you decide to go with first)

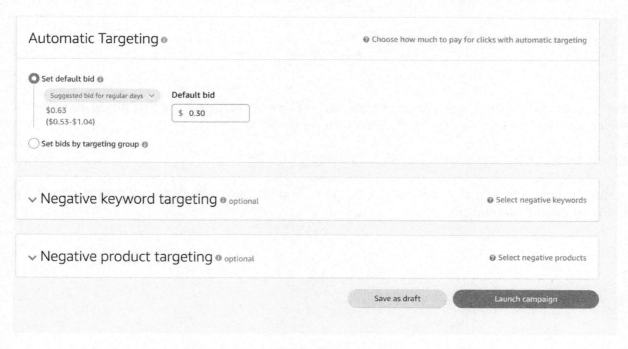

Once you scroll down, it will ask us what we want to set our default bid for the automatic campaign. I usually always start off with $0.30 and adjust it accordingly once I have enough data. For the first week to ten days, though, $0.30 will be perfect.

That is the end of the auto campaign, don't click on "launch campaign" yet. Click on "save as draft," as it makes sense to revise them all at the end before submitting your ads for review.

The next campaign that we will launch is the manual campaign.

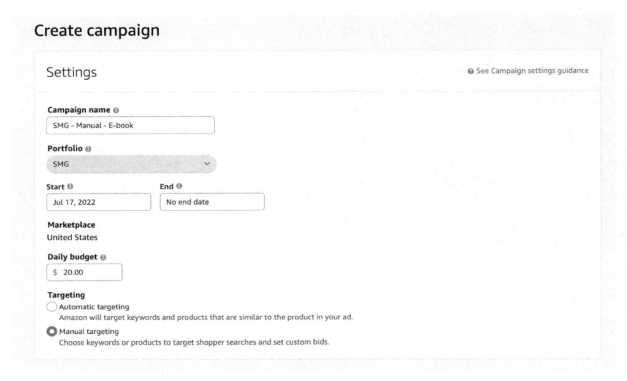

Again, I do the same thing with the campaign name. The only difference is that this will be for the manual campaign. Also, make sure the right portfolio is selected.

The daily budget will be the same for all. $ 20 a day will suffice.

This time around, because it is a manual campaign, you will need to click on "manual targeting" and not "automatic targeting."

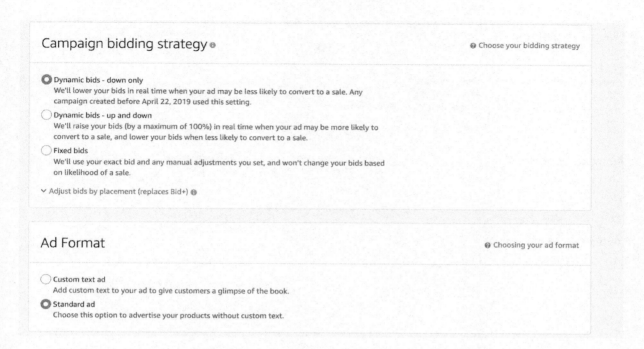

The bidding strategy will be the same for all our ads; dynamic bids – down only.

I also tend to go with a standard ad. However, this is a matter of preference. Just make sure that you select dynamic bids down only for the bidding strategy.

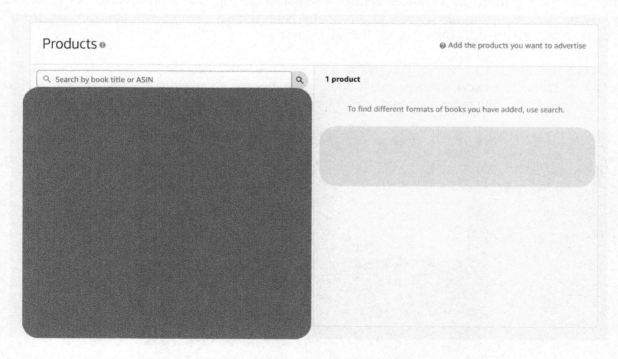

Again, make sure you select the right book that you want to advertise.

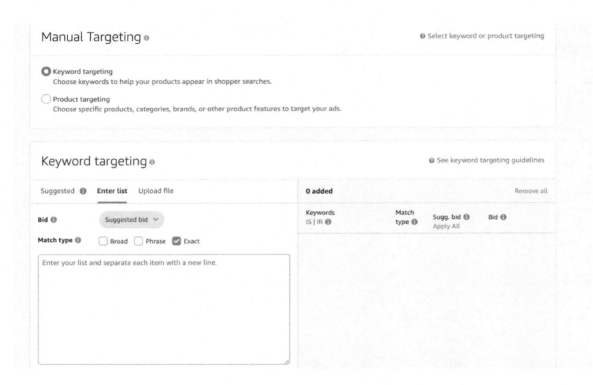

When it comes to manual targeting now, select keyword targeting, then click on enter list. For the match type, I like to have it on "exact," meaning that the keywords will be exactly matched to what I enter here, giving no room for interpretation for amazon to suggest similar phrases or a broader look. Again, this is just my preference. There really is no right or wrong with amazon ads. It's all based on seeing what works for you and sticking with it.

Then click on enter list. Now, you want to copy here the search targetwords and author targetwords from your excel spreadsheet. It does not matter which targetwords you enter first. Just make sure you enter both the author and search targetwords.

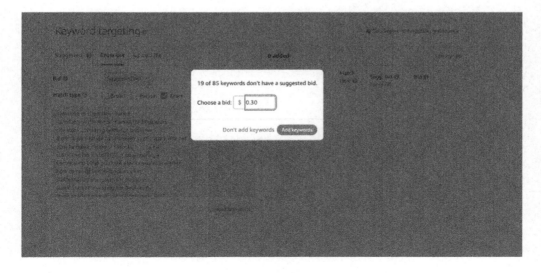

You will then be shown a pop-up like this when you click to add your keywords. Amazon here is asking you to set a bid. Again you can change it to $0.30, as the default will be $0.75. then click on add keywords.

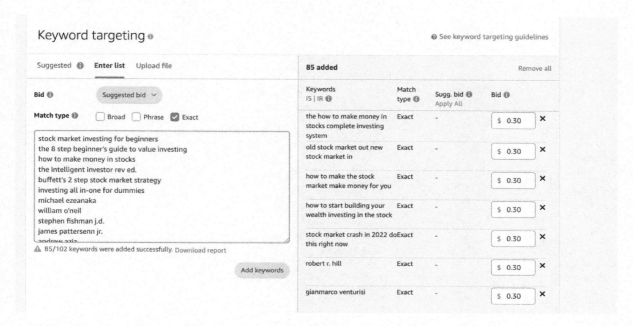

Now, as you can see, your keywords will show as "Added" on the right-hand side. One thing you might notice is that not all of your keywords or targetwords will get accepted, this is totally normal, and you should definitely expect a few to not go through. The reasons are unknown. However, it does not impact your campaign at all.

Also, note that the example above shows 85 added keywords. However, for your campaign, you will have about 250-300. This was an example to show you how it works.

Again, scroll down and click on save as draft for now.

Let's now move on to the next type of campaign. This is the ASINS campaign. There will be two types of ASINS campaigns that we will run. One is the ASINS categories, this type of campaign targets the categories that your book would fall under. The ASINS exact is a campaign where we copy the ASINS of our competitors, these are the ones that we got from publisher rocket, and you should find them under the ASINS targetwords.

Let us start with the ASINS categories campaign. Again, make sure you click on sponsored products campaign and click on continue.

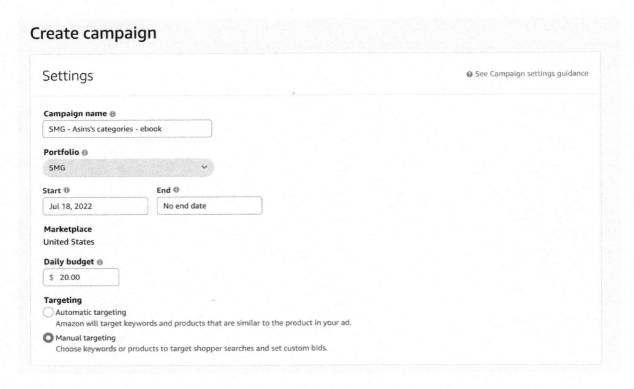

It will be the same as the other campaigns. The only difference is that we will name this one as. "ASINS categories' on the campaign name. The budget and target will remain the same. $20 a day and manual targeting.

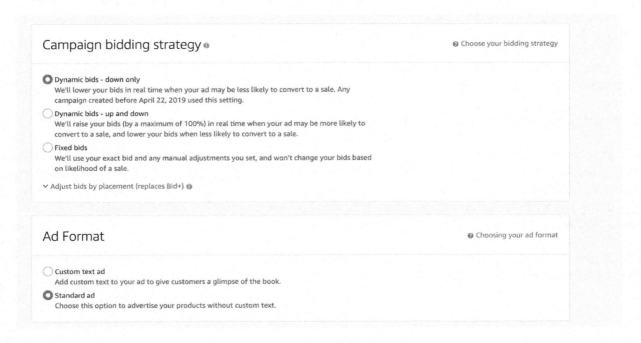

The campaign bidding strategy will be the exact same as well. You can choose a custom text ad or a standard ad. I prefer a standard ad.

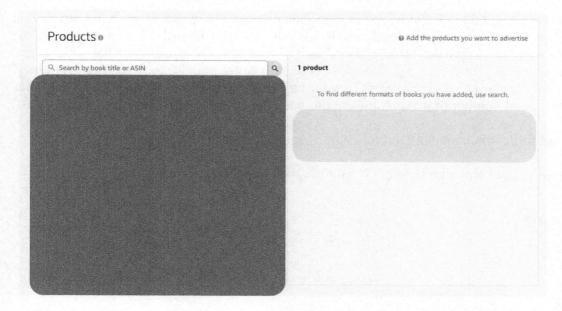

Again, make sure you select the right book that you want to advertise.

This is where things will slightly differ for the ASINS category campaign.

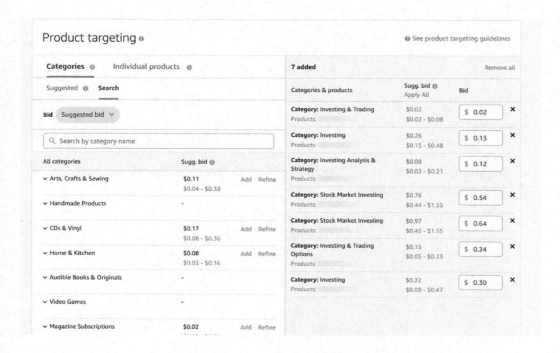

You want to make sure you are selecting product targeting, unlike keyword targeting as we did for the manual campaign.

On the product targeting tab, make sure you move to the categories section, then go to search. You want to search for amazon book categories that are relevant to your title. For example, in the above, the title was "stock market for beginners" as you can see, the categories that were added were relevant to that keyword. For e.g., I added "investing & trading," "stock market investing," etc. You want to add ones that are relevant to your keyword. Try to add at least 7-15 categories here, so we get a good number of impressions on our ads when they launch. Save the ad as a draft.

Make sure to not forget to change the bid for each category to $0.30.

Now let's create the last campaign before we multiple them for the paperback book.

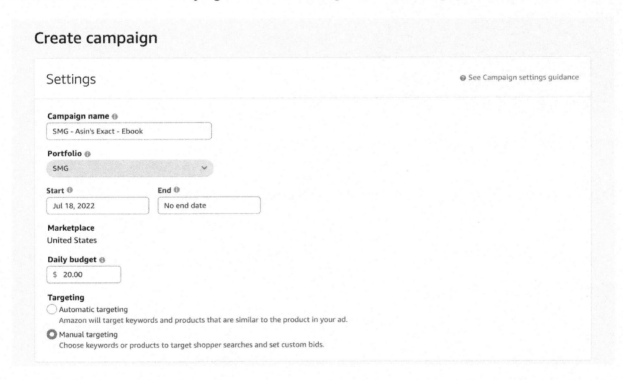

This will be the last campaign; this one is the "ASINS exact" campaign. Again, the settings here are the same. Same budget, manual targeting.

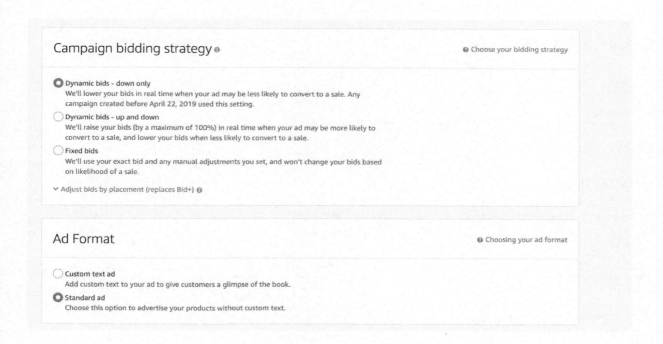

We will also use the same bidding strategy and ad format.

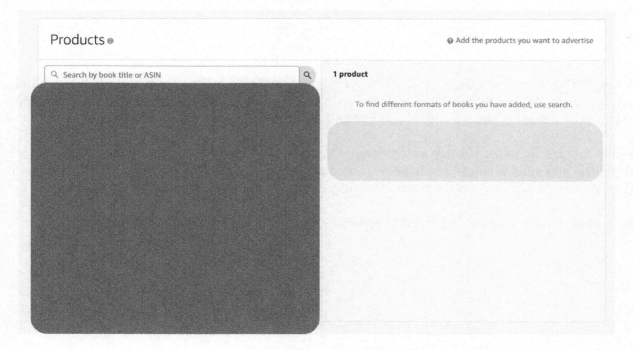

When you scroll down again, make sure you add the book that you want to advertise.

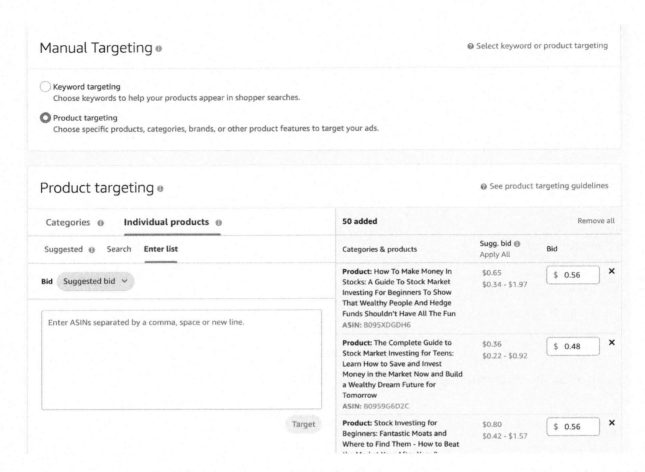

For the ASINS exact campaign, we will be on product targeting for the manual targeting method. However, instead of being on the category section like we did on the ASINS categories campaign, we will go to the tab of the individual product and then click on where it says "enter list."

As you can see, it will then ask you to enter the ASINS. You will then go back to your excel spreadsheet and copy them. Come back over here and paste. Once you have selected all the ASINS and they show as "Added" on the right-hand side, do not forget to set a default bid of $0.30.

Again, make sure you select "save draft" and don't hit the "launch campaign" button just yet.

Now, as you can see, we have the manual e-book campaign, the auto campaign, the ASINS categories and the ASINS exact. Right now, there are four campaigns. You would need to create these again, but for the paperback version.

If you are on a budget and cannot afford to do another four campaigns, I would recommend that you do four only, but for the paperback and not the e-book. This is because the royalty that you will earn from your paperback is higher than the e-books.

Before you launch the campaigns, make sure you have done everything right, then hit the "launch campaign" button.

Monitoring your amazon ads

You need to let your AMS ads run for ATLEAST 7-10 days. We leave it for this long to be able to collect data from our ads to make wise decisions going forward.

What is the difference between optimizing and scaling your ads?

Optimizing – trying to make something more efficient while following the same steps.

Scaling – doing more of what is already working but at a much higher budget.

Rules to follow in general

• If your campaign has a lot of impressions but little to no clicks, consider changing your cover/refreshing it.

• If your campaign has a lot of impressions and clicks and no sales, it might be something to do with your book description. Fresh it up.

• If neither of the above work, try to make some changes to your TOC or the formatting of your book.

Rules to follow when optimizing

• If you have less than ten clicks – let it run for another week. Don't make any changes to your targetwords.

• If you have 10+ clicks and 0 sales – Consider pausing the keyword.

• If you have 10+ clicks & an ACOS over 40% - decrease the bid by $0.02 - $0.03

• If you have 10+ clicks & an ACOS between 30% - 40% increase the bid by $0.02 - $0.03

• If you have 10+ clicks & an ACOS between 20% - 30%, increase the bid again by $0.02 – $0.03

• If you have 10+ clicks & an ACOS less than 20%, then increase your bid by $0.05 - $0.10

Rules to follow when scaling

• Another way to increase the number of impressions and exposure for your campaign is to increase your daily budget.

• Once you have a successful campaign of 30% ACOS or less, then you want to adjust your daily spending by $5 every 2-3 days.

• If you continue to see more sales, gradually work this up. Remember, it is all about testing and seeing what works!

• Perhaps try to also raise the price of your book and see if the sales stay consistent. You could be taking more royalties and not knowing.

• If you have tested different covers, tried different book descriptions and even made some changes to your interior, it may be time to pause that campaign.

If you have adjusted your bids accordingly and tried new and fresh targetwords, it may also be time to pause that campaign.

• Sometimes amazon ads just don't work… nobody knows why. Try to switch off the ad and create the same campaign again. This sometimes has a positive impact.

With your amazon ads, it is totally normal to break even or even make a loss during the first month of a new book launch, contrary to what you may have heard. It is important that if you see your ads breaking even after the first week or two, to keep running them. As I mentioned previously, the first 30 days of your book launch is when you want to generate as many sales as possible as Amazon wants to see how well the book will sell. If your book is breaking even after the first month, but you show Amazon that the book is making consistent sales, they will be more likely to favor your book over competitors in the search engine, in the long term, you will make more royalties and sales if you keep your ads switched on.

Chapter 8: Bundles

Bundling on amazon and audible is offering multiple books in one, also sometimes referred to as a "value set."

Bundling is a very good tactic to maximize your sales on KDP, especially on audiobooks.

This is also why I highly recommend that you go for a niche where you can write at least 3-4 books so that you can bundle them together later on. Bundling only works well when the book bundles are all linked to a series or are on the same topic/keyword.

There are two ways in which you can create bundles on KDP and ACX.

The first way is to create a series of books and bundle them together.

For example:

Book 1 – Python programming for beginners

Book 2 – Python programming for Intermediates

Book 3 – Python programming for advanced learners

The second way is to bundle books that are not part of a direct series but are closely related.

For example:

Book 1 – Python programming for beginners

Book 2 – Java programming for beginners

Book 3 – C++ Programming for beginners

Both can work very well, although based on my personal experience, I have found that bundling books that are part of a series works the best and yields the best results.

What do I need to create an eBook bundle?

Before you go and create your bundles, there are some rules that you must be aware of that KDP has stated for bundling.

Some things to take into consideration:

• When it comes to e-books and paperbacks, you can make as many bundles as you want. (As many combinations as you like)

• With audiobooks, you can bundle one book once, but after that, you can't use the book in a bundle again.

• Because of this, you should publish your largest (in length) bundles to ACX and keep the shorter ones for KDP.

Now that we have that out of the way let me explain how you can successfully bundle e-books first, then I will explain for paperbacks.

To bundle your e-book, you need to:

• Step 1 - Create a new word document

• Step 2 – Copy and paste the content of each e-book you want to bundle in this file.

• Step 3 – Make sure the fonts, sizing, and colors of the different texts match each other

• Step 4 – Remove any redundant section. For e.g., you only need one copyright disclaimer page at the beginning of your bundle.

• Step 5 – Create a brand-new TOC for your bundle.

• Step 6 – Come up with a new bundle title. It should still have your main targeted keyword. However, it should be clear from your title that your book is a bundle. You can do this by having, for e.g., 2 in 1 at the start, or 3 in 1, etc.

When it comes to creating a new table of content for your bundle, what I mean by this is that you should have a hyperlinked table of contents that will take the customer to the start of each book in that bundle.

For example, if you have two books in a bundle, your bundle table of contents that the customers would see at the start of the book would look something like this.

Table of contents

Book 1

Book 2

It would be hyperlinked, meaning that if they clicked on "book 1," they would be taken to book 1, and likewise for book 2. This is the easiest way to do it and the most convenient for the readers. I do want to clarify, though, that just because we have one table of contents for the bundle, that does not mean that the table of contents for each book will be removed. No, they will still be there, but we just add the bundle table of content as it is a quick and convenient way for the readers to get to whichever book they want in the bundle, without having to scroll down all the way to book 2, for example.

To get a hyperlinked table of contents page like the above, you would simply highlight "book 1" and "book 2" and select a heading for them. I like to go with heading 3. Whichever heading you are going to choose, make sure it does not conflict with the headings used for the table of contents in the book. It has to be a separate heading, only for the table of contents for the bundle.

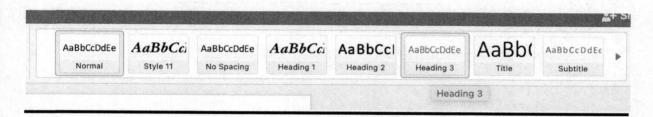

Once you have done that, now what you will need to do is go to the title page for each book in your bundle, simply type "book 1" on the title page for the first book, and make sure you label that with the same heading that you did on the table of contents for the bundle.

You would also do the same for the 2nd book in your bundle, go to the title page, write "book 2" under the title and label it with the correct heading. Once you have done this, you are ready to create the hyperlink.

To create the hyperlink, go back up to the table of contents of the bundle, highlight both books 1 and 2, and then just like you can see in the picture, once you have highlighted them both, click on index and tables.

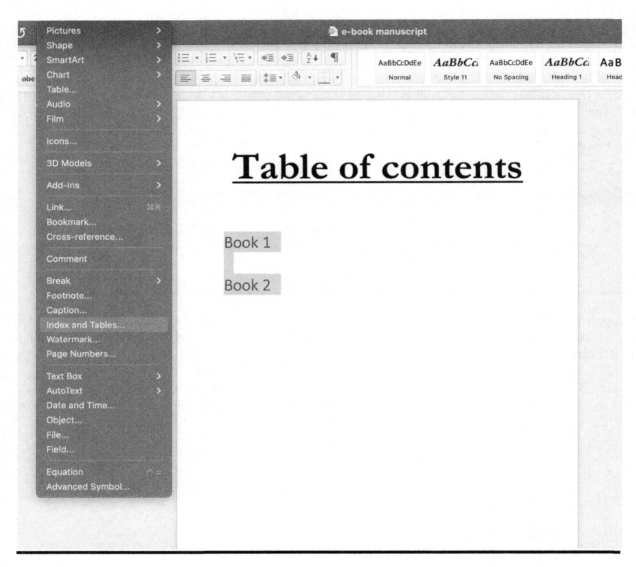

By default, you will be taken to this page. You can click on "table of contents."

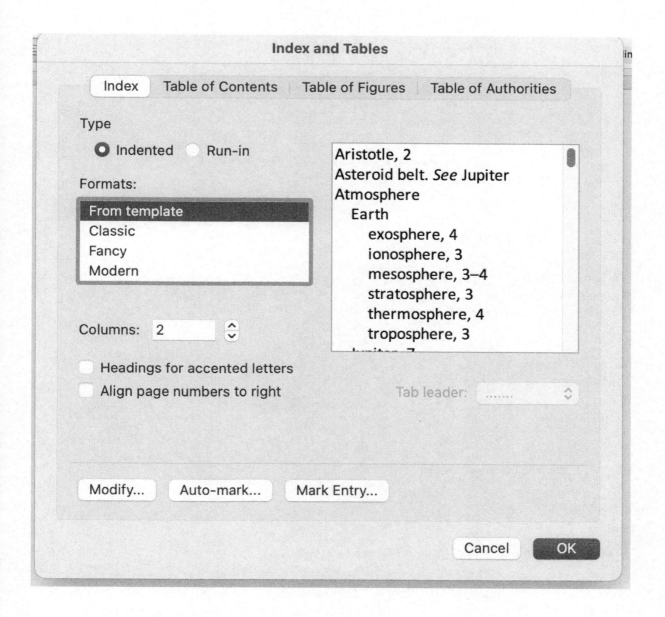

Once you are on the table of contents, click on "options."

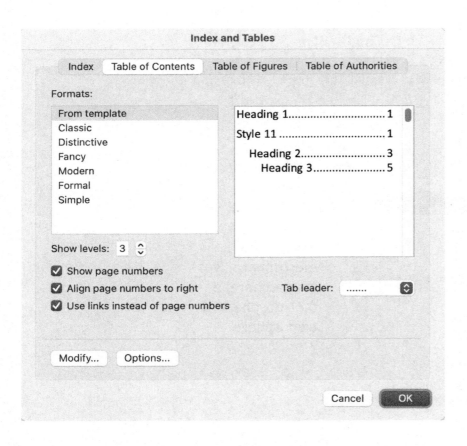

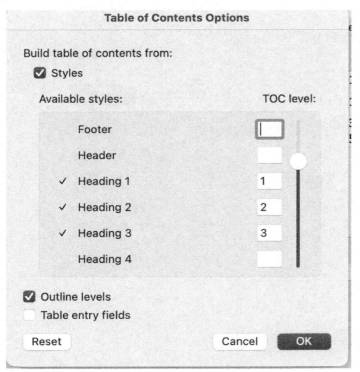

By default, it should look something like this, you need to remove the number 1 in heading 1 and remove the number 2 in heading 2, so in the end, it should look something like this.

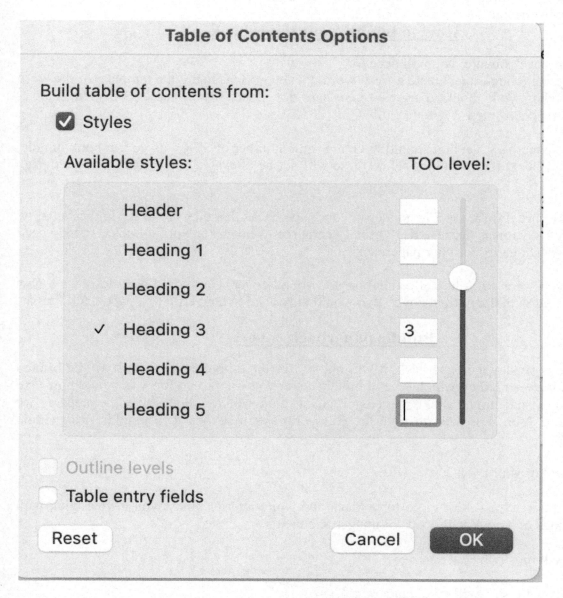

Then click on okay. There you have it, your own distinct table of content for your bundle.

Bundle covers – e-books

There are two types of covers that you can go with for the e-book bundle.

The first one is collective covers. These usually come in the form of a box set. The second way to do it is to include all the covers in one cover

Both are fine. It's a matter of preference. I prefer the second option. Whichever option you go with, you will need to get a brand-new cover design made for your bundle. To create the bundle cover for your e-book, it shouldn't cost you more than $10. Make sure you explain your requirements well to the graphic designer.

How to bundle your paperback

To create a paperback bundle, you will need to:

• Step 1 – Like the e-book one, create a fresh word document (make sure the template of the word document matches your book margins– you can download blank copies of them here - https://kdp.amazon.com/en_US/help/topic/G201834230

• Step 2 – The paperback version should have the same number of TOCs as your e-book bundle, with one main TOC at the beginning. Note these will not be clickable and instead will have page numbers.

• Step 3 – Make sure if there are any images in your paperbacks that they are of the highest quality, the reason why I say this is because KDP usually compresses images in your e-books, so they need to be of the highest quality for your paperback.

• Step 4 – If you went with the collection/box set e-book cover, you would need to order a new cover. If you went with the normal cover, you would only need to convert it to a paperback format.

Bundle paperback covers

For the bundle cover for the paperback, it will not be like the e-book because this will be printed out. Once you have settled on which type of bundle cover you want to go for, you would now take that e-book cover and turn it into a paperback cover. You would follow the same steps as we discussed before. You will need to give the following specifications to a graphic designer on Fiverr/Upwork:

• The page count of your book

• The ink and paper type – best to go for a black and white interior unless you have a book with many illustrations or a book with loads of images and charts.

• Trim size – will mostly be 6 x 9 or 5 x 8

• Paperback cover finish – will it be matte or glossy?

• The blurb description – I usually take this from the book description; however, you can come up with something new if you would like to.

• Is there something specific that you want to be written on the spine?

How to price your e-book bundle

What has personally worked best for me is when I:

• Make it a 3 for the price of 2 types of deal or 2 for the price of 1.

• Like this, customers will have a clear incentive to get the bundle instead of buying each e-book individually.

• For e.g., if you have three e-books in your bundle, and they cost $2.99 each, price the bundle at $5.99

• I typically price my e-books at $4.99 each, so if you have three e-books in the bundle, price the bundle at $9.99

How to price your paperback bundle

A general rule of thumb for paperback bundles is to add an extra $4 to the price for each book that is included.

• So, if your standard paperback is $13, you will sell the bundle of two for $17

• If it's a 3-in-1, you will sell the paperback bundle for $21

• If your paperback is $14, you will sell the bundle of two for $18

• If it's a 3 in 1, you will sell it for $22

However, this is not set in stone, and you should experiment with the price. It all comes down to your cover quality, reviews, and the niche you are in.

Audiobook bundles

Before we get into audiobook bundles, at this stage, I am assuming you have already posted the audio version for each individual book on audible. If you have not, then you must do that first.

There are now only a few things you need to do:

• You need to pay a narrator to record new opening and closing credits for the new bundle title.

• You will still need to upload each opening and closing credits for each book.

• Get your new cover re-sized for ACX (2400 X 2400 PIXELS).

Once you have these ready, it's time to claim your book on ACX and upload your files as you usually would.

Chapter 9: An Introduction To Audible, Royalty Structure, And Sale Types

Audible is an Amazon-owned business. They are the market leader for audiobooks. Audiobooks make up more than half of my income from my publishing business. In this chapter, I plan to explain why I think audible is such a good opportunity in 2022 and beyond.

Firstly, unlike with Amazon KDP, audible does not have an ad platform, meaning that all sales that are generated on the audible platform are pure profit. If you do a good job with SEO and you get your book to rank for the keyword, you will make sales for years and years to come. The best part about this is that it is completely passive once you get a few reviews on your book.

One thing to note about audible through is that they are currently only open to residents from the UK, US, Canada, and Ireland. This is unfortunate if you are outside of these places. However, it presents a brilliant opportunity if you are a resident within.

To create an audiobook for your paperback, all you will need to do is create an ACX account via acx.com. If you already have an Amazon account that is linked with your KDP account, you will automatically have an ACX account, so it is super easy.

Another thing that I love about audible is the lack of competition. With KDP, a lot of keywords are very competitive and almost impossible to compete in, whereas with ACX, there is a huge ocean of opportunities waiting for you to explore.

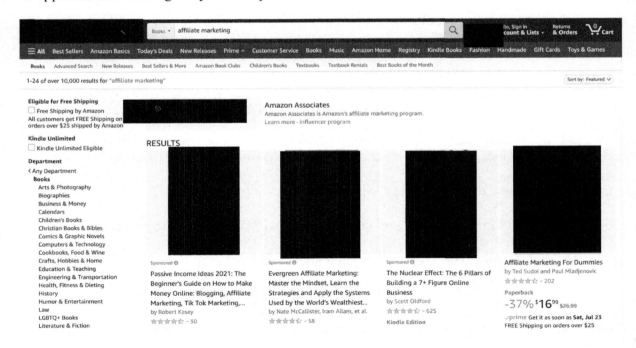

For example, if we search for the keyword "affiliate marketing" in the book section on Amazon, you can see there are over 10,000 competitors for this keyword.

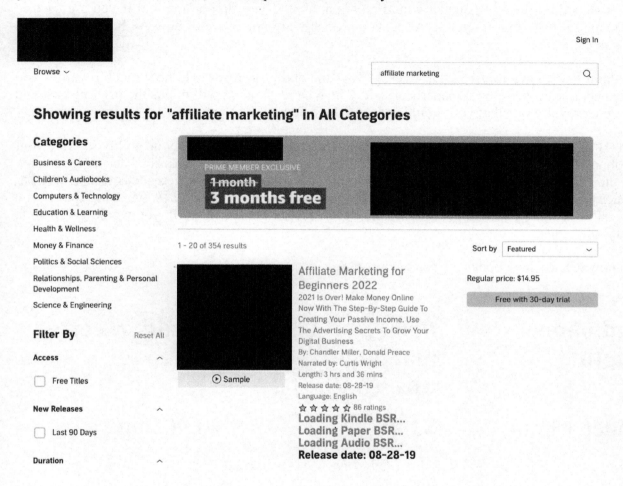

However, when we search for the same keyword on audible, there is a lot less competition, with only 354 audiobooks on the topic.

ACX is the backend profile to audible. It is the platform where you will upload all of the audio files for your Audiobook. Once you submit them on ACX, they will go through a review period that can take ten business days. Once your book has passed the review period, it will be live on the audible platform.

Your Audiobook will be available for purchase on Amazon, audible, Apple music & iTunes, so you will have plenty of organic eyeballs on your book. It is simply your job to produce a high-quality book that customers will want to buy.

ACX royalty structure

This is something that I thought I would mention, as it is very important, and if you are used to publishing on KDP but not yet on ACX, you probably are not aware of how ACX works in terms of royalties.

One thing that I have to give KDP over ACX is the clarity in regards to how much royalties you can expect to earn per e-book/paperback sale. The KDP dashboard will minus the printing cost and give you a royalty rate that you should expect to take home.

With ACX, this is unfortunately not the case. For starters, you do not have the ability to price your audiobooks how you like, as you do with KDP books. Instead, books are priced according to how long they are in narration. I will explain this in just a second. Another difference is that with ACX, you get paid 30 days after a sales period, whereas with KDP, it is 60 days. Meaning that if you make sales in June, you will get them at the end of July, whereas on KDP, you would get them at the end of August.

Let's now discuss how books are priced on ACX.

Audiobook length	Price of audiobook at this length	Royalty received
Under 1 hour	$3.95	$0.90 avg
1-3 hours	$6.95	$1.80 avg
3-5 hours	$14.95	$3.4 avg
5-10 hours	$19.95	$4.4 avg
10-20 hours	$24.99	$5.40 avg

20 hours +	$29.95	Not sure

As you can see from the above table, the longer your book is, the more it is priced and the more royalties you will receive for a sale.

This is why I recommend getting your book to at least 3 hours long because if you do, you get almost double the number of royalties compared to the royalty category below it. A 30,000-word book should help you to get your book to 3 hours long in audiobook format, so aim for 30,000. You can also do it with 25,000 – 27,000 if you get your narrator to repeat a few things like bullet points or narrate certain parts of your script slower than others.

Now that you know the royalty structure, it is also important to discuss the type of sales you can expect on ACX. There are three types of sales on ACX:

• AL units – This is where a member of the Audible membership purchases your Audiobook using membership credits (membership sales). This is where the majority of your sales will come from. You get roughly 20% royalty from these

• ALOP units – This stands for Audible listener off-plan member. This is when a member does not purchase your Audiobook using credits. You get roughly 28% royalty from these.

• ALC units – This stands for A La Carte or a non-member purchase. This is when a customer purchases your book outside of their membership at full price. This is the sale type where you get the most royalties. Roughly 40% royalty from these.

• Bounty – When you tell friends or family about your book, and they sign up with audible using your book as a free trial, you receive a $50 bounty.

Most of my sales are AL unit sales, and that is why in the above table, I listed the "average" royalties you can expect. These are the royalties that you should expect in the scenario of an AL unit sale. If you get any other type of sale, you should expect more.

Chapter 10: Audible Keyword Research And Narration

In this chapter, I will explain my methodology and approach when it comes to doing keyword research for audiobooks.

For starters, you will not need to buy any more tools, so if you have got the KDspy tool from using it during keyword research for KDP, that's perfect, as we will be using it again!

However, you will need to download a free google chrome extension called BSRmaster. This extension will tell us the BSR rank of the audiobooks on audible, which is very helpful!

For audiobook keyword research, we will create a different excel spreadsheet. Our judging criteria for the profitability of a keyword will also slightly differ.

Keyword	Does the keyword have 100 results or less?	Is there more than 3-4 reviews with over 50 reviews?	Is the book suitable in audiobook format	Is the Avg BSR 30/40k for the first page

The first column is nice and easy. Just copy the keyword you are researching in this section.

The second column asks us if the keyword has 100 results or less on audible.com (make sure you are on the .com site and not any of the others)

If you can remember, with KDP, we were aiming for results of 4,000 or less. Due to how much less competition there is on audible, we look for keywords that have results of 100 or less, it's okay if the keyword has a little over 100, but it shouldn't have hundreds of results for that particular keyword. 100 is a realistic amount of search results to be able to compete with and rank your book on the first page. Remember, the aim is to get your book to rank on the first page. If we are able to do that, we will likely get a lot of audiobook sales, provided that the niche is in demand. Type "Y" for yes in the spreadsheet and "N" for no.

The third criteria that we will look for are if there are 3-4 books on the first page of our keyword that has over 50 reviews. If this is the case, it might be a difficult keyword to compete for because your competitors already have a huge leg up on you with their great feedback. If there are 1-2 books on the first page with over 50 reviews, and the others are below 50, this is a really great opportunity! Again, type "Y" for yes in the spreadsheet and "N" for no.

The fourth criterion that we take into consideration is if the keyword is suitable in audio format or not. The truth is that some books are more suited to audio, whereas others are more for print. For example, it wouldn't make much sense to make an audiobook for a cookbook or a workout book, that is because these keywords are more centered around images and step-by-step illustrations. Most keywords will be suitable for audiobook format; however, you must ask yourself if your keyword is suitable or not. If you are not sure if your book makes sense in audio format, ask your sibling or friends for their opinion and take it from there. Select "Y" for yes if your book makes sense in audio format and "N" for no if it does not.

The last criteria for my ACX keyword method are to make sure that the first page of your intended keyword has an average BSR of 30-40k. If you remember, I said you should look for 150k and less for KDP. For ACX because the competition is so much less, we need to lower the average best seller's rank to ensure we get consistent sales of our audiobooks.

How you would find out the BSR of the first page is by using the KDspy tool, they have recently added the feature for audiobooks, which is very helpful. However, the tool does not work if you try to use it directly on audible. Instead, you will need to search for the keyword on Amazon (make sure you are on the books option), then click on the KDspy tool, and click on the audiobook icon. This will tell you the avg BSR of the first page of your keyword. If the avg BSR is slightly above 40k, but all the other criteria are very good, I would still definitely recommend that you go ahead with producing the Audiobook. The ideal situation is to find a keyword that is profitable on both ACX and KDP. However, this is unfortunately not always the case. You may sometimes only find a keyword that looks really profitable on KDP but non-existent on ACX and vice versa.

Fill out your excel spreadsheet with as many keywords as you can. In the end, choose which keywords you want to go ahead with and produce your Audiobook.

Let's now talk about the narration for your Audiobook and the different options at your proposal.

Audiobook narration

When it comes to audiobook narration, there are two main options. The first option is to find narrators through the ACX marketplace. They have hundreds of thousands of different narrators, and the process of finding one for your project is very simple. You would simply display your book open for auditions once you have claimed it on ACX, then expect about 10-20 people to apply to the audition.

ACX

There are some advantages and downsides of finding narrators through ACX. Let me explain.

One of the main advantages of going directly through ACX is that there is not much vetting to do, compared to going through Upwork. You simply choose the narrator who you think suits your book, and you work with them. All of the narrators on ACX have to follow a standard procedure in terms of quality, so you know you are in safe hands and working with people who have professional audio equipment. Unfortunately, the same cannot be said for Upwork.

Another great advantage of finding a narrator through ACX is that ACX has now started asking authors for copyrights of the books they wish to get narrated before they can find a narrator. This is great for the narrator because it means they don't have to deal with the headache of narrating a book that violates the rights of another and, in turn, does not get paid. This, unfortunately, has happened a lot in the past with ACX narrators in their marketplace. However, this problem is now getting tackled very quickly, and for the betterment of narrators too.

Another great thing about narrators on ACX is that they are very well aware of ACX requirements when it comes to audio. ACX has its own set of requirements when it comes to accepting audio files. For example, they will need a room tone level of a certain level. The book should have opening and closing credit files. The audio should be a specific RMS number, etc. Because narrators on the ACX platform have narrated a lot of other books, they are well aware of these requirements, and they will usually send you back the files correctly the first time, which will save you some valuable time. This is unfortunately not always the case with Upwork.

However, there are some major disadvantages, in my opinion, of finding narrators on ACX. One of the biggest ones is that the prices of narrators are usually fixed in their bio, and there is usually little to no space to negotiate with them. The prices for narrators on ACX are displayed in brackets. The lowest one is $50-100 per finished hour. Per finished hour is not every hour that the narrator spends on recording your Audiobook. It is every finished hour of your Audiobook.

This is the lowest rate you will find on ACX, and it can very quickly become a lot more expensive if you want to work with narrators who have a high reputation.

Also, if you go through ACX, I have realized that the communication is often not as good with the freelancer as compared to Upwork. It may be that the freelancer is not as active on ACX as they were, or the system has been set up in a way that makes communication more difficult.

Another downside to ACX is that narrators, for the most part, submit the final Audiobook when they have finished the narrating and editing and then want to be paid. This can be overwhelming for you as you would have to listen to hours of audiobook narration while the narrator is waiting to be paid. On Upwork, I usually work chapter by chapter with my narrators that way. It gives me plenty of time to listen to each chapter, and I don't have to rush my review and assessment of the work of the narrator.

I do also want to mention that when you want to find narrators on ACX to narrate your new book, they will give you the option of paying the narrators either through per finished hour, meaning that you pay them a fixed rate per finished hour of your Audiobook. So, if your Audiobook was 3 hours long, and you agreed to a per-finished hour rate of $50, you would be paying them $150 in total for the Audiobook.

On the other hand, they also have the royalty share option. This means that you pay the narrator nothing upfront, and they produce your audiobook upfront free of charge. However, the catch is that they will receive half of your royalties for the next 7-8 years of that book being published. I am hugely against going through royalty share because you could be losing out on a lot of money. For example, if you produce a high-quality book that becomes a best-seller, you will have to half your royalties from that book with the narrator every single month!

If you don't have the funds right now to find a narrator, I would recommend you save up until you do. It is honestly not worth going the royalty share route. I feel like this way of paying narrators has been created to benefit narrators, but not us, the authors. Stay away from royalty share!

Upwork

In regards to Upwork, I find most of my narrators through there instead.

One of the main reasons why I prefer Upwork to the ACX marketplace for narrators is that you have a lot more flexibility to negotiate the final price that you are willing to pay for your Audiobook. Remember that you are the one who is posting the job listing on Upwork, you can make the requirements as you wish, and that also includes the price. On ACX, as I said, prices are fixed, and I have generally speaking found the narrators not willing to budge on those prices or certain other requirements such as the time span of finishing the Audiobook.

I have found that I can save at least $50-60 if I go through Upwork compared to the ACX marketplace, which really adds up if you are doing a few audiobooks.

Another great thing about Upwork is that the narrators on there are generally speaking very active and responsive, you can reach out to them any time through Upwork messenger, and they will get back to you as soon as they can.

Furthermore, you have full control and power in regards to how you want the freelancer to send you the files and how long you want them to take to narrate the whole book. It is very common to get a finished three-hour audiobook in as little as two weeks with Upwork. Also, I like to work chapter by chapter with my narrators, meaning I ask them to send the audio files of each chapter as they finish it, and not all at once in the end. This is to make the review process for me a lot easier and not overwhelm me.

One of the downsides of Upwork is that the platform is not necessarily vetted. Yes, you can see the feedback of a freelancer on their platform, but that is not necessarily the reality of the situation, especially with audiobook narrators, because they usually do a few other things on Upwork too. This means that it is your job to vet out each candidate that applies to your audiobook posting. The questions that I ask each candidate before I start working with them are:

- Which audio equipment do you use?

- Are you aware of ACX audiobook requirements?

- How long would it take to finish my book?

The reason why I ask about audio equipment is for me to make sure they are using a professional microphone. As surprising as it sounds, I have had plenty of freelancers in the past who have tried to work with me while using the voice memo app on their iPhones. These are things you need to be very well aware of. Don't be shy to ask which equipment the freelancer uses! Remember that your book will be live for sale forever, so you need to do it right from the start to have a consistent stream of sales.

I also ask if they know ACX audio requirements because, as I have already mentioned, ACX do have its own set of requirements, and I have found that a lot of audio narrators on Upwork are not aware of them. This means that they have to then search for them and try to do things right the first time. Usually, they do not get it right the first time, and there is a few back-and-forth with the narrator, although this, for me, is worth it due to the amount of money you will save in the long run. If this, however, is a deal breaker for you, you can go directly through the ACX marketplace, and you should expect to have your audio files right the first time.

I also ask how long the freelancer would take to finish the narration of my book so I can set the expectations right from the start and so there is no pressure on the side of the narrator to work faster than they can. It is a good idea to ask whether you are going through Upwork or the ACX marketplace for narrators.

How to know which narrator to choose

Choosing a narrator can sometimes be a challenging and time-consuming task. I take the following criteria into consideration when choosing a suitable narrator.

• Your narrator's gender should (generally speaking) match the gender of the pen name. This is done to match the congruency of your Audiobook.

• Your narrator's voice/tone should match the tone of your Audiobook. Would you want a female narrating a survival book? Or a tough, gritty voice narrating a children's book?

• Avoid using AI or a robotic-sounding narration.

• It all comes down to your preference. You decide whether the narrator suits your book or not

Good audio vs. bad audio

Audio quality is important because:

• It will hugely affect sales.

• A good quality narration shows professionalism.

• The lifetime sales will last longer.

• You will get better reviews with better quality audio – it does happen!

Good audio will:

• Be clear and crisp

• Have no background noise

Bad audio will:

• Not be so clear

• Either too loud or too quiet

• Small background noises

Chapter 11: How To Publish Your Audiobook

Okay, at this stage, you should have chosen which marketplace you will use to find your audiobook narrator, and hopefully, you should have chosen one by now.

The question is, will you give the same e-book manuscript to your narrator and tell them to start narrating?

The answer is no. Your manuscript will be slightly different as there will be some things that you need to add in the form of instructions.

I like to include a blank page in my manuscript that I give to the narrator for my book. I usually write this on the first page:

Notes for my narrator

'There will be some text in this manuscript that is colored red. If you come across text as such, these are not to be read out loud and are for instructional purposes only.

Please feel free to correct any small spelling or punctuation mistakes that are not detrimental to the comprehension of this book. If you come across a bigger mistake that needs my attention, please do let me know. This book has been proofread multiple times; however, it is likely there are things we missed out on.

Please understand that you are not to narrate the table of content or the copyright page. Therefore, I have removed them from the original manuscript.

Each chapter will have its own audio file. Please remember that the Audiobook has to be narrated and edited to ACX requirements. If you are not aware of them, you can find them here **https://www.acx.com/help/acx-audio-submission-requirements/201456300**

In addition, I will also need a separate opening credit file and a closing credit file.
In the opening credit file, you will narrate the title and subtitle of the book, written by the author (myself) and narrated by yourself (your name)

For the closing credits, it will be the same with the addition of "the end."

If you have any additional questions or concerns, then do not hesitate to contact me on ACX/Upwork.'

Having a note like this before the main book is very important, especially if you are working with a narrator from Upwork because chances are they won't already know the above information.

I make it clear to the narrator that they are not to narrate the table of content and copyright page.

I also let them know that each writing in red has instructions for how I want them to be narrated.

For example, if you are creating a workbook for kids and want the narrator to narrate certain activities and exercises slowly, you will highlight the activity in red, then what you want to do is add a comment on Microsoft word by the activity to reinstate your objective. Doing things this way makes it extra clear to the narrator how you want things to be done. Add a comment for any small requirement you may have, as it will save you a lot of time and hassle later on when you are listening back to work.

Review plug

I also have a review plug somewhere around three-quarters into my book. A review plug is simply asking listeners to review the book. We put this in around 75% into our book because, at that time, the customer would have had enough time to write a fair and honest review. Anything before is not enough for them to leave a review.

I will ask the narrator to read out something like this at the end of chapter 6/7

'Hey! I apologize for interrupting. I just wanted to see how you're finding [BOOK TITLE] so far? I'm excited to hear your thoughts on it!

If you could spare 30 seconds to give a quick review on Audible, even if it's only a sentence or two, that would be fantastic!

And don't worry, this Audiobook will not be interrupted.

To do so, go to your Audible app and tap the three dots in the top right corner of the screen, then tap the "Rate and Review" icon.

This will lead you to the "rate and review" page, where you can give the Audiobook a star rating and write a few sentences about it.

That's all there is to it!

We're excited to read your feedback. Leave us a message since we read every review personally!

Now let's take you to step by step through the process.

Simply unlock your phone, tap the three dots in the upper right corner of the screen, then select "Rate and Review."

Simply enter your star rating, and you're done! That's all there is to it.
I'll give you another ten seconds to finish sharing your thoughts.
——- Wait for ten seconds. ——-

Thank you so much for taking the time to write a quick Audible review.
We are very grateful since your feedback is really valuable to us.

Now back to your Audiobook.'

This is a very nice way of asking our listeners to leave a review on our Audiobook on audible. A plug like this works very well, and I have gotten a dozen of organic reviews solely by using this method alone, so don't underestimate it and make sure you include something like this in your book.

Uploading your book onto ACX

At this stage, you should have got your audio files back, and you are almost ready to upload your Audiobook onto ACX.

Before you go ahead, you will need to get your cover made for Audiobook. The dimensions that were used for the ebook and paperback will not work for audiobooks as audiobook covers are a lot smaller.

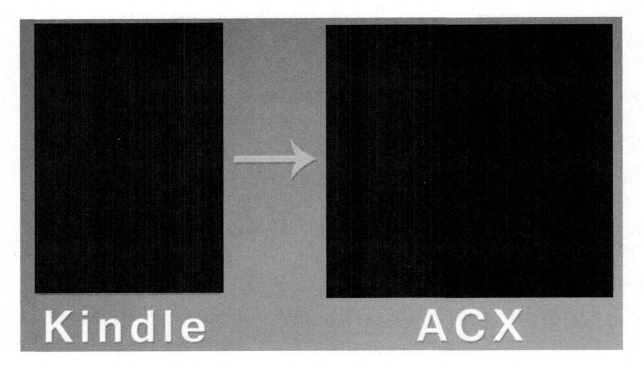

As you can see from the image above, that is the difference between the e-book and ACX cover.

You will need to buy a gig on Fiverr from someone who specializes in turning ebook covers into ACX covers.

You will send them your kindle cover and ask for an ACX one, make it clear to the freelancer that the dimensions for the audiobook cover are 2400 x 2400 pixels.

Once you have this, it's time to upload your book onto ACX!

Log into your account on acx.com.

Then click on where it says "Add your title."

Start by searching for books from your catalog.

Showing results for:

[🔍]   [Search]

We are searching Amazon.com for your book based on the keywords above.

Search Tips

You can only start the audiobook creation process if your title is listed on Amazon.com.
Please ensure the spelling of your name and/or title is correct.
If you still can't find your title, or it is available only on Amazon sites outside the US, please contact us and
include your title's ASIN and whether you already have completed audio or plan to find a producer on ACX.

It will take you to a page that looks like this. Type in the title of your book or the ASIN, and it should appear here. Note that you must publish at least your e-book on KDP before you are able to claim the Audiobook. There is no other way around that. So even if you are only focusing on audiobooks, you must at least first publish the e-book.

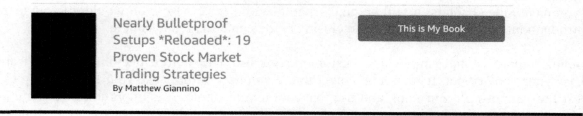

Nearly Bulletproof
Setups *Reloaded*: 19
Proven Stock Market
Trading Strategies
By Matthew Giannino

[This is My Book]

When your book then pops up, you will click on the purple button that says, 'this is my book.' You will then be asked if you want to search for a narrator to narrate your book or if you already have the audio files ready to be uploaded. Hopefully, at this stage, your files will be ready, so click on the latter option.

You will then be asked to fill in some information. Make sure you opt for world rights to your book and not US or UK. This means that your book will be distributed worldwide to other audible marketplaces as well as the UK and US audible platforms.

The next one is very important; they will ask you how you want to distribute your book. You can either go exclusive and receive a 40% royalty rate, meaning that you can only publish your book to audible, or you can be non-exclusive, meaning you can publish your book to audible and other audio aggregators, and receive a 25% royalty rate. Because audible are the market leaders for audiobooks, most of the sales come from audible anyway, so I have found that going exclusive is by far the best option. If you have your book exclusive for one year, and it doesn't make the greatest number of sales, you could switch it to non-exclusive, but for the first year, keep it exclusive.

2. Copyright Information *

Please specify the copyright information associated with your print book and audiobook. If there is more than one print copyright year, please specify all of them. This information is typically read in the opening and closing credits of the audiobook.

Print Copyright Owner	Print Copyright Year(s)	Audio Copyright Owner
	2022	
↑ Pen name here		↑ Pen name here

You will then be asked to write your copyright information. For the print copyright owner, make sure you write it as your pen name of the book and not your personal name, the same for the audio copyright owner.
You will then be asked to choose your category. Make sure you select non-fiction for your book and then choose the category which best describes your book.

After this, you will be taken to the upload manager on ACX. This is the section where you will upload the audio files for each chapter. Remember that you can only upload one file per chapter, so if you have nine chapters, it will be nine separate audio files. Also, you would, of course, need the introduction, conclusion, opening and closing credits, and the retail sample.

The retail sample is the sample that customers can listen to before deciding if they want to purchase your book or not. It cannot be longer than 5 minutes. Simply ask your narrator to pick out the best few minutes of your book and use that as a retail sample. It is important that you choose the best part of your book because it will dramatically increase the number of sales. Remember that this is the only preview that customers can listen to before making their decision, so you want to leave the best possible impression on your customer.

Full Production – 3 hrs 8 mins 20 sec*

*Current running time, which does not include the retail audio sample

Manage the audio files for your finished production below.

There will also be an audio analysis tab next to the upload manager. It will have a red logo by the side if there is anything wrong with your audio files. If there is, it allows you to download a neat excel spreadsheet with any mistakes the narrator might have made when editing the audio. Simply give that to them, and they should fix the problem for you very quickly.

If everything seems fine and there is nothing wrong with the files, submit your files. You will then get a message to say that your book has been submitted for review and that this process can take ten working days. It is usually completed before that. However, it can take up to 10 working days.

Title change + Superpower email

Once your Audiobook is live, you may want to request ACX to change how your book is displayed, this is for SEO purposes, and not a lot of people know about this, but it is totally legal to do.

By default, audible will only display your title and hide your subtitle in the main title.

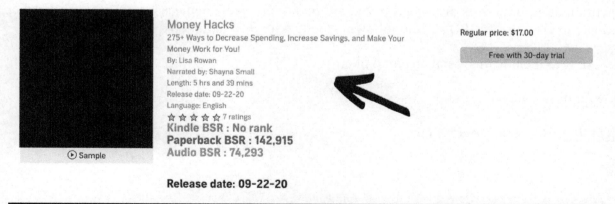

It will look something like this. The title is Money Hacks. The subtitle is 275+ ways to decrease spending, increase savings and make your money work for you.

You can actually ask ACX to include the whole title and subtitle on the main title, this can massively help you with SEO, so when a customer searches for one of the keywords in your title, your book will show up.

To get ACX to change this, simply send an email like this:

ACX Email: support@acx.com

Subject line – Title change request

Body

Hi!

Could you please change my audible title listing? Currently, it is displaying only the main title (ENTER MAIN TITLE HERE), and I would like it to also display my subtitle (ENTER SUB TITLE HERE)

So just to confirm, I would like my book title to be displayed as (NOW ENTER TITLE & SUBTITLE TOGETHER)

Another thing that you can do is get your Audiobook to have the PDF of your book in the customer's library. It will look like this on the audible book listing.

PLEASE NOTE: When you purchase this title, the accompanying PDF will be available in your Audible Library along with the audio.

This is a great incentive for people to buy your book over competitors because I very rarely see the competition doing this. It is also good if you are in a niche like language learning, as the listener would like to also read the PDF while following along with the Audiobook.

To get ACX to include this, send an email like:

ACX Email: support@acx.com

Subject line – Complimentary PDF

Body

Hi!

I would like to add this ebook/paperback PDF to the customer's library after they purchase my book.

(TITLE & SUBTITLE HERE)

I have attached the PDF of my book.

Once ACX has received your Email, it shouldn't take more than a few days for this to be visible in the audible product listing. This should boost your sales over time, so please make sure that you do it, it takes minimal effort, but the rewards will be huge over time!

Chapter 12: Audiobook Promotion

Once your Audiobook is live, it is now time to start promoting it like crazy! Getting reviews on your Audiobook is nowhere near the same amount of stress as it is on KDP. ACX gives authors something called promo codes. These are free codes that authors can distribute to their friends and family, so they can listen to your book for free and they can leave a review.

ACX will give you 25 codes for the UK marketplace and 25 codes for the US marketplace. As I said, you can distribute these with your friends and family, so you should be able to distribute them relatively quickly.

Sales Dashboard   Earnings Report   Promo Codes

To find your promo codes, simply go to your sales dashboard, then you should see them on the right-hand side.

Remember that the people you are distributing the codes to must either be in the US or the UK, and they must also have an audible account. They must also listen to at least 75% of your Audiobook to be able to leave a review.

I am confident that you will be able to distribute the majority of these codes through your network, but if you end up having a few left, let me explain how you can distribute the rest effectively.

Social media groups

The first place that I would look if I had some leftover codes would be Reddit and Facebook groups. You want to join a group in your niche, start interacting with people and let them know that you have a free audiobook, trust me, people will reply and take an interest because everybody loves a freebie. Just make it clear that you want a review in exchange and that they must be from either the UK or the US for it to work effectively.

Freeaudiobookcodes.com

The second thing that you could do is to list your book on free audiobook codes. This is a website that has a large user base and email list of passionate audiobook listeners. How it works is that you pay $12 to have your book listed on their website in the correct category, you will tell them how many codes you have left for each marketplace, then they will list your book for free, so anybody will be able to redeem a code, listen to your book and leave a review.

The only thing with free audiobook codes is that you can't vet out who redeems your code and their history in regards to leaving a review. It could well be a possibility where people redeem your code and listen to your book but do not leave you a review, which is a shame.

For that reason, I only recommend you to go through this route. If you have already tried to redeem all of your codes and you have just a few left, then it is fine.

<u>Don't do this!</u>

You might come across a few gigs on Fiverr or Upwork of freelancers who claim that they will redeem all of your ACX codes and leave positive reviews on your book. Don't buy these gigs. This is not allowed with ACX and can lead to your account being terminated.

My final request...

Being a smaller author, reviews help me tremendously!

It would mean the world to me if you could leave a review.

If you liked reading this book and learned a thing or two, please let me know!

It only takes 30 seconds but means so much to me!

Thank you and I can't wait to see your thought.

Conclusion

I hope you have enjoyed this step-by-step guide on how to build a profitable self-publishing business. I honestly believe that publishing is one of the best opportunities for beginners online in 2022. You do not need thousands of dollars to get started, you do not need to store any products, and you can start this business from anywhere in the world!

Self-publishing is a very legitimate business that can, over time, replace your 9-5 income. I have recently sold my publishing business for close to 6 figures after working on it for the last year and a half.

People seek publishing businesses to buy because of how passive they are and the little maintenance that they require once the work has already been put in.

Audiobooks are by far my favorite side of publishing. Audible presents a brilliant opportunity due to the lack of competition and the huge pool of keywords that are yet to be explored on the audible platform. I believe that it is very realistic to build a 6-figure business with just audiobooks, so please do not overlook audiobooks because the market for them is only increasing year over year!

Please understand that self-publishing is a business, and with any business, it does take time for you to be successful. Don't expect your first book to be a best seller in the book department. It is possible but probably unrealistic to have that as an expectation. I say this because you will probably break even or even lose money during your first 2-3 months when you are running your ads. You have to trust the process and understand that publishing is a long-term business. Your books will make you money for years to come, so don't be hasty and switch off your ads immediately if they don't seem to be profitable from the start.

Publishing is a very lucrative business model and can be truly "passive income." Thank you for reading this book, and I wish you all the best in your publishing endeavors.

Resources

https://www.amazon.com/Developing-Emotional-Intelligence-Capabilities-Successful/dp/1775009459/ref=sr_1_1?crid=13W79WIGMULCC&keywords=developing+emotional+intelligence+30+ways+for+older+teens&qid=1663285329&sprefix=developing+emotional+inteligence+30+ways+for+older+te%2Caps%2C600&sr=8-1

https://www.amazon.com/EQ-Applied-Real-World-Emotional-Intelligence/dp/3981984110/ref=tmm_pap_swatch_0?_encoding=UTF8&qid=1663285410&sr=8-1

https://www.amazon.com/Overthinking-Improving-Self-Esteem-Meditation-Toughness/dp/B09CCHBYMS/ref=tmm_pap_swatch_0?_encoding=UTF8&qid=1663285460&sr=8-1

https://www.amazon.com/Stop-Overthinking-Techniques-Declutter-Emotional/dp/B08XLLF3PG/ref=tmm_pap_swatch_0?_encoding=UTF8&qid=1663285487&sr=8-1

https://www.amazon.com/Emotional-Intelligence-Leadership-Business-Self-Awareness-ebook/dp/B07WRHWWF2/ref=sr_1_1?crid=12RHPRHULZ36U&keywords=emotional+intelligence+for+leadership+improve+your+skills+to+succeed&qid=1663285545&sprefix=emotional+intelligence+for+leadership+improve+your+skills+to+suc%2Caps%2C383&sr=8-1

https://www.amazon.com/Emotional-Intelligence-Modern-Leader-Organizations-ebook/dp/B0875QJ1XS/ref=sr_1_1?keywords=emotional+intelligence+for+leadership&qid=1663285569&sprefix=emotional+inteligence+for+leader%2Caps%2C340&sr=8-1

https://www.amazon.com/Why-Does-He-That-Controlling/dp/0425191656/ref=tmm_pap_swatch_0?_encoding=UTF8&qid=1663285598&sr=8-1

https://www.amazon.com/Power-Discipline-Control-Toughness-Achieve/dp/B086PRLDCB/ref=tmm_pap_swatch_0?_encoding=UTF8&qid=1663286147&sr=8-1

https://www.amazon.com/Empowered-Empath-Boundaries-Controlling-Emotions/dp/1093401834/ref=tmm_pap_swatch_0?_encoding=UTF8&qid=1663286197&sr=8-1

https://www.amazon.com/Cognitive-Behavioral-Therapy-Techniques-Depression/dp/B087R3WGTC/ref=tmm_pap_swatch_0?_encoding=UTF8&qid=1663286276&sr=8-1

https://www.amazon.com/Highly-Sensitive-Emotional-Overload-Eliminate/dp/1720622493/ref=tmm_pap_swatch_0?_encoding=UTF8&qid=1663286328&sr=8-1